SECOND HELPING

Newfoundland Labrador
Nunavut and Travels Beyond
....a memoir..

John P. Christopher

Order this book online at www.trafford.com
or email orders@trafford.com

Most Trafford titles are also available at major online book retailers.

Cover photo: View of entrance to St John's harbour from Signal Hill (Atlantic side).
Back cover photo: View of Freshwater Bay from Signal Hill *and* photo of the author.

Print information available on the last page.

ISBN: 978-1-4907-8253-9 (sc)
ISBN: 978-1-4907-8255-3 (hc)
ISBN: 978-1-4907-8254-6 (e)

Library of Congress Control Number: 2017907564

Trafford rev. 06/09/2017

 www.trafford.com

North America & international
toll-free: 1 888 232 4444 (USA & Canada)
fax: 812 355 4082

Contents

Background

The Arctic Circle----Cosmic or Oblique Geometry

The arctic circle (66 degrees 33 minutes north of the equator), as defined: .... that time of year (the date) when the earth in its orbit around the sun has the sun 24 hours a day in the northern hemisphere....commonly known as the summer solstice..........and along any point on that circle and to the north of it on that date there is total light. Arctic Day.

In cosmic geometry terms, when the angle of the earth's tilt (its obliquity) is subtracted from 90 degrees at this line we get 23 degrees 27 minutes; and 66 degrees 33 minutes north latitude is the number of degrees north of the equator.

Also at this line (the Arctic Circle) and to the north of it 6 months later we are in total darkness........ (Arctic Night), these dates represent the shortest and longest days of the year. Dec 21 and June 21 on the calendar in the Northern Hemisphere.......

Conditions are just the opposite on these dates in the Southern Hemisphere.

The Arctic Ocean is almost land locked and surrounds the Arctic Circle. The Arctic region is an ocean surrounded by continental land masses while the Antarctic region is just the opposite, a continental land mass surrounded by ocean.

Surviving in the Ocean: A modern example of Darwinian evolution. [For those interested: there is a short but relevant Darwin biography available by the author as well.]

Man continuously wants to see himself as separate from the rest of the world of natural forces, something that he alone can control, not the reverse. Perhaps it's as simple as being unable to truly comprehend the very long time over which nature takes to work its magic i.e. truly appreciating the fact that the universe itself is some 13 and ½ billion years old. In over the two and a half million years that we've been around (geologic and evolutionary time are very slow moving forces) a lot can happen to alter the original model. Yet, there may be instances when change can be brought about more quickly, which seems to be going on in our own time, with regard to climate change. Witness the dramatic changes due to climate that have begun to alarm us in just the past few decades alone, prominent among them being the carbon levels in today's atmosphere that have gone from 316 ppm in the 1960s to today's alarming 400 plus ppm.

Not all of this excess carbon is absorbed by the ocean (only about a third is). To go along with the soaring atmospheric and oceanic carbon levels we have accompanying global warming: via satellite imagery we now see a startling melt of Arctic Ocean ice cover and dramatic melt of glacier ice sheets in Greenland and elsewhere resulting in a rise in ocean water levels and concomitant erratic weather patterns.

In a special case, sudden evolutionary change may even be looked at with special relevance in today's diminishing fish populations worldwide, and in particular to the collapse of North Atlantic cod stocks on the Grand Banks. The cod, an otherwise tough midsized omnivore predator, will, when it first becomes "aware "of threats to its survival from overfishing, begin to make adjustments in a number of ways, as do all living creatures, the most apparent of which in the cod is to come to sexual maturity at an increasingly early age, when it is a much smaller animal. In its attempt to avoid pending extinction, the northern cod has seen its sexual age of maturity halved in the last 40 years or so from a normal 6 or 7 years to a present age of just 3 or perhaps 4, as well as also a much lower reproductive rate. When forced to start reproducing themselves at this younger age, the egg laying potential of the young animal drops off markedly from about 9 million eggs (as was the case just 40 years ago), in normal large, fat, old, female cod…usually five and six footers in length…..the rule here being, the older the animal, the more fecund she is), to today's perhaps 1/100th or even

$1/1000^{th}$ that number of eggs. Other, less dramatic changes in the northern cod's behaviour might involve migration to a new ecosystem entirely, one with a different water temperature or even migration to a new water depth. Evolution works to maximize the number of descendants an animal leaves behind. Recent massive overfishing i.e. increasing the death rate of the fish, leads to evolution favouring maturity of younger and smaller fish.

Nature is the ultimate pragmatist as Darwin notes, continuously experimenting with various combinations of environmental factors until something is found that works. This is all quite incredible really; all we need do to see this phenomenon in action is to behold the ubiquitous cockroach or in the case of flora, the common weed. Many are invasive species, both fauna and flora that have been successful in finding new homes for themselves where they can survive and even thrive; all are crafted by evolution into skilled opportunists, species not fussy about who they mate with or where they have to live.

Prologue

Why there're no Cod on the Grand Banks today

The Task Force on Incomes and Adjustments in the Atlantic Fishery, chaired by Rick Cashin, an old classmate of the author's and onetime president of the Newfoundland Fishermen's Union, issued the concluding statement in 1993:

"Too many harvesters, using too many boats, (of all kinds), with too much gear, trying to supply too many processing plants, by finding and catching too few fish."

This statement summed up nicely the sorry state of the Grand Banks Cod Fishery, i.e. overcapitalization by government (s) and overfishing by all participants, one year after the federal government had been forced to declare a moratorium, effectively closing down the fishery, in 1992. A healthy 500 year old sustainable cod fishery on the Banks had survived, broadly speaking, until the early 1950s. Interestingly, this decade also marks the end of the famous Portuguese White Fleet, 50 strong, to the Grand Banks fishery, restarted in the mid- 1930s after an absence of almost 400 years. These 3 masted Portuguese barkentines employing principally sail, (though they also had small backup auxiliary motors) used the old fashioned way of catching cod: the baited hook and line that had allowed the fishery to survive for as long as it had.

The Marine Stewardship Council lists three principles that consumers of fish should look for when making their purchases.

1) sustainability of species
2) habitat damage or danger to other species
3) Good management procedures i.e. well regulated

The exploitive 250 year old Newfoundland, in shore fishery Truck system.

A few words are in order here to acquaint the reader with the fishing on credit or Truck system that was created for fishermen in Newfoundland's outports, possibly as early as the 1780s or 1790s, when an in-shore fishery gradually replaced the off-shore migratory fishery that had lasted for several hundred years. Using this system the fish merchant didn't pay in cash but gave credit on goods purchased in his dry goods store. He set the price for the fish he paid in the fall and charged for the goods that he sold in his store to the fishermen along with a markup. It made for a near feudal economic system existing in the late 19th century and early 20th century.

This in-shore fishery with its credit system persisted almost right up until modern times. Some say it was the only way that commerce could have evolved where it did, along an almost endless coastline, encompassing as it did many hundreds of small, isolated settlements. Others condemn it outright as the systematic oppression of a voiceless people. At root, an abuse prone system, in the end it served neither fisherman nor merchant. It basically was kept in operation by the local fish merchant in an outport or by an agent of much larger St. John's Water St. merchants, supplying the fisherman each spring with all he wanted or needed to engage in the fishery for the coming year, in regard to nets, lines, hooks, anchors and the like, with payments made by the cod landed (and cured) in the fall. The merchant set the prices and paid the fisherman for the fish as he saw fit, the fisherman having no say in the matter. The merchant set the price not only for the fish landed but also for what goods the fishing family might need from the shelves of his store to get through the coming winter and spring, this could include everything from nails and putty to flour, sugar and molasses. If the year was good, more goods might be obtained, if bad, the fisherman's family could be left to the mercy of the merchant. Would they be given extended credit or would they have to go without, during the coming winter? The system was essentially cashless, resulting in no independence for a family that was forever beholden to the merchant, being always in a state of constant and continuous subservience.

The migratory fishery had flourished from the early 17th century, with many thousands of fishermen setting out for the Grand Banks from Cornish ports like Cornwall, Bristol, Poole and others every spring, to spend the summer fishing, and after filling their ship's holds, to return home again in the fall. The system also in time, came to be relied on by the British Navy as an on-going source of trained seamen. That is, until the ongoing 30 years of the American Revolutionary and Napoleonic Wars, when fishermen became unavailable to travel annually to the Banks fishery in great numbers. Starting at first with just single or pairs of fishermen, but soon followed by other family members, people over time, made the decision to overwinter in Newfoundland, with many staying on, and an in-shore fishery gradually took root. Amazingly, the population of the Island grew to 50,000 between 1785 and 1815 and soon a summer Labrador fishery using Newfoundland based schooners from the north east coast was begun that greatly expanded over the years.

The outcome of the American Revolution presented a number of challenges for Britain. For one thing, she was now cut off from a source of cheap quality oil, oil that had previously been plentiful from the large New England whaling industry, oil essential for lighting, lubrication and the curing of leather, all of which were becoming increasingly important to Britain's burgeoning industrial revolution. Seal hunting, an activity that in Newfoundland until then had only been familial, and pursued chiefly as a food source, became by 1810 a major industry, employing many thousands of fishermen and hundreds of ships during the down fishing months of early spring, March and April. Especially valuable was the oil of baby harp seals (white coats). The personal income earned during the hunt, anywhere from $40.00 to $80.00, if lucky, often became the difference between starvation and survival for a family.

Sealing

"Tis jest a dog's work while it lasts, but somehow there's an excitement in it, that sets young fellers kind o' restless in the spring….a man, 'll go for swile where gold won't drag 'un." A quote by fishermen John Saunders in Newfoundland and Her Un-trodden Ways 1907.

The industry itself was known as swilling (sealing) and between the 1830s and 1930s it occupied the minds and bodies of 20 thousand or more Newfoundland sealer/fishermen and 400 vessels, usually half the male population between Notre Dame Bay and Trepassy Bay. During the peak years of the 1840s an astonishing 500,000 seal pelts would be taken annually. For comparison, during the same period, fur seals in the north east pacific were hunted to near extinction. The business of sculping (flensing) the seal pelts took place there on the ice floe. Here, if the herds were plentiful, a large mound of pelts would soon be built up, to be picked up later by the sealer's mother ship. Sealers habitually risked their lives but accepted it without question. The experience of a trip 'to the ice' (usually understood to mean 'the front', a large area lying off the North East coast of the Island but also to a lesser degree the Gulf of St Lawrence), was not to be missed, rough and dangerous, it became to be regarded as a rite-of-passage for young outport Newfoundlanders. All one needed for the hunt was a gaff, (a wooden pole about 6 ft. in length, with an iron spike and hook attached at the end, a suitable flensing knife and a 10 to 12 ft. length of sturdy hemp rope for towing seal pelts along the ice. All aspired to get 'a berth' aboard a sealing vessel, be it schooner in early days or later larger barks ("wooden walls") or in modern times, large steamers, ("ironclads"), built for maneuvering in ice. Crew sizes might vary anywhere from 40 to 275, (when men would be packed in like sardines) depending on vessel size and construction. Grub tended to be sparse, even meager, generally not much more than bread and butter, duff, brewis and tea, and seldom even potatoes. Protein only came when the vessel was actually 'in the fat' and men were permitted to return to their ship with their own seal flippers which were then cooked up by the ship's cook for a "good scoff" all around. Most sealers made a few extra dollars by selling these flippers to St. John's town folk at dockside at voyage's end, which could be anything from a few weeks to a couple of months in length. Flippers were usually the only seal body parts, (along with the pelts) taken aboard for personal sale and use. The flippers were cut off at the time of flensing (sculping) and put aside for later pick up. The rest of the carcass was left on the ice. I can only surmise that polar bear populations were healthy in those days.

In the 19th century before the days of steam and iron, the ships (schooners and barks primarily), were referred to as "wooden-walls" whereas, after the turn of the 20th century, and after most sealing vessels were constructed of iron they came to be called "iron-clads".

The merchant vessel owners charged the sealer for a berth, a "signing- on" charge to go to 'the ice' until 1902, when there was a 'sealer's riot' in St. John's. Although it was squashed, it did lead before long to the elimination of a number of exploitative practices in the sealing industry, of which charging for a berth to the ice certainly was one. Sealing was a hard currency earner for poor inshore fishermen of Newfoundland's outports where cash was very hard to come by in the oppressive medieval "Truck" system of fish trade.

In modern times many reforms were introduced by the Canadian Government, of which, most importantly, was the highly controversial white coat hunt which was banned in 1984. Just a few years later, in 1987, the 'large vessel' hunt to the ice fields itself was also banned. Of course the EU's banning of the importation of all seal products in 1984 had a huge impact on the industry, practically obliterating it, with only a modest land based hunt for local hunters now existing.

Molasses Bread and Tea was the memoir book I put out many years ago, that dealt almost exclusively with highlights of my employment with the Fisheries Research Board of Canada, Arctic Unit, from 1961 to 1965. It included in some detail, the traditional Newfoundland seal hunt as I experienced it aboard the Canadian -Norwegian sealer and arctic research vessel M V Theron under Capt.

Harald Maro during the 1961 and 1962 seasons. As well, it detailed a couple of summers I spent camped out on the tundra when collecting beluga whales for the FRB at Whale Cove, District of Keewatin, now in present day Nunavut.

FRB, was then an arm's length, quasi –independent and world renowned research facility. [It has been defunct since 1974, when it was closed down by the government of the day for being perhaps a little too critical of what had been up to then official government policy. Its staff was then absorbed into a newly revamped Department of Fisheries and Oceans].

But by this time we can assume that the government knew full well that just around the corner lay its enactment of the 200 mile EEZ also in 1974, (Exclusive Economic Zone), which would ban foreign vessels i.e. the large modern factory trawlers of these nations, from fishing on most of the Grand Banks, thereby ostensibly eliminating overfishing of the cod stocks from that foreign source. But the reality was what followed. Overfishing of the cod stocks simply continued as before, by even larger and more modern trawlers than before, the only difference being that they were now Canadian owned. Perhaps the thinking simply was, better we get rid of the FRB critics in advance. Molasses Bread for the most part, covers my years as a collector of marine mammal specimens for the FRB's Arctic Unit in Montreal.

I spent several summers (1962-1964) in the company of Inuit hunters on the west coast of Hudson Bay, working from the recently created Inuit settlement of Whale Cove, (circa 1960). My collecting season of beluga there lasted from mid -June when the ice left the cove until early September, at first signs of freeze up. The unforgettable and rather gruesome seal hunts lasted aboard Theron from the end of February until early May. In 1965 I decided to return to university and registered at U of T in a PhD programme.

Sealing became another way to earn scarce dollars for a people desperately hanging on, and sometimes it meant the difference between life and death for families that barely survived in isolated outports through the long bitter months of winter with scarce food sources. The industrial scale seal hunt also came to fill the otherwise "unproductive" months of March and April along the north-east coast, when heavy coastal ice conditions for all intents and purposes closed down the fishery until late April. The Hunt, as I said above, came to be regarded as a rite of passage for Newfoundland outport youth, perhaps beginning as early as 14 years of age, and before long it became an Island wide tradition. An activity that before 1790, had only been family based, grew within a single generation, to become a major occupier of the Island's male workforce. It had come about as a result of the successful American Revolutionary Wars in the 1780s, a result being that England became cut off from a previously steady source of quality whale oil, a commodity desperately needed for lighting, heating and the just beginning industrial revolution.

The massive area of surface sea ice drifting south off Newfoundland and Labrador, called the "front" during sealing days, annually becomes the breeding grounds to millions of harp seals each spring. Here they haul out on the floes to give birth and mate. In anticipation of these breeding behaviours, thousands of sealers would gather in St John's at this time of year, in hopes of "winning" a berth on one of the sealing vessels bound for the 'front'.

Seal hunting was a dirty, difficult and dangerous job for little pay, (sealers, being regarded as individual entrepreneurs, were paid in shares of the catch, i.e. not salaried employees, from which their clothing and rations were also subtracted, where the sealers might also have to pay for a berth fee to become part of the crew as has been noted above. The sealers took their highly coveted berths aboard sealing ships for the duration of the voyage, usually from 4 to 8 weeks. Sealing was a highly labour intensive occupation, often leading to grossly overcrowded sealing ships, often with crews of 150 men or more.

For my trips to the seal hunt, in 1961-63, I was extremely lucky to be aboard the M.V. Theron. Her owners, the Karlsen Shipping Co., had a special arrangement with the federal government, whereby gov't scientists were given facilities aboard ship to carry out their research; chart the Arctic Ocean's floor, map the Archipelago's c coastlines, collect their specimens for study, analyse water samples etc. Theron was a special and very classy vessel of her day. Just a few years before my coming aboard, in 1956-1958, she and her mixed Norwegian/ Canadian crew of 25 or so men, had taken Mt Everest summiteer Sir Edmund Hillary and Brit explorer Sir Vivian Fuchs, the co-leaders of the Joint British/ Commonwealth Transantarctic Expedition's (TAE) Advance Party, along with 24 sled dogs, 8 Snow cats, 8 other smaller arctic tundra cats and several Ferguson tractors, along with spotter Auster aircraft, to Antarctica. From the continental ice shelf of Antarctica in the Weddell Sea, (Shackleton Base) the first successful crossing of that continent via the South Pole was begun in 1956 by the advance team and others. With this knowledge I needed no further inspiration while aboard Theron to endure whatever hardships might be encountered. For inspiration I had only to close my eyes for a moment at night to realize that just scant few years before, Fuchs and Hillary were also here in this this same cabin and sleeping in these same bunks.

Working with the Inuit in Whale Cove, I was busy almost daily, extracting canine teeth for aging later in the lab from local beluga catches. I too had put out several large mesh nets with my Inuit helpers to capture beluga and inspected the nets almost daily. From both seals and whales I sometimes collected other organs as requested, including reproductive organ, stomach contents and even fetuses and seal skulls if these were also on the shopping list given me by my employers. For the harp seal samples, these tasks could only be filled when the ship was working among the huge herds as they lay on the ice floes (i.e. when we were "in the fat", in the Newfoundland vernacular). The collections on Theron eventually filled several large steel barrels and numerous wooden boxes, dozens of glass jars and hundreds of vials.

Death on the Ice

I once heard an outport relative speak when he was in his eighties of the circumstances surrounding one of Newfoundland's greatest sealing disasters. He was among the SS Newfoundland's crew of sealers at the time of the tragedy and had first- hand knowledge of what happened during the more than two days that the storm raged and the sealers wandered lost out on the ice and how they attempted, many in vain, to keep themselves alive. He was one of the lucky ones who survived to tell the tale.

Before they were eventually picked up on the morning of the third day, 78 men of the 150 had perished.

"It was an awful time bye, I can tell ya."

He was generally reluctant to speak about the nightmare he'd gone through, but with the help of a couple of drinks of rum to relax the mind and lubricate the tongue he could be persuaded.

There were actually two major sealing disasters that occurred during that same late March 1914 storm. By some strange confluence of celestial or oceanic and atmospheric conditions they occurred in the same year, the same month, the same day, and at very nearly at the same hour, separated only by 400 km as the crow flies. The other shocking loss was that of the SS Southern Cross that occurred just hours before my story teller's own ordeal on the ice began. The Southern Cross was perhaps half way back to St. John's with a bumper load of 40,000 or more harp seal pelts, from their breeding grounds on the pack ice that had been channeled via the Strait of Belle Isle into the Gulf of St Lawrence, when disaster struck. In the absence of any other reasonable explanation it's thought she likely was probably greatly overloaded but we'll never know for sure just what happened.

She, as had many other sealing vessels at the hunt that year, been stripped of her wireless by the owners before sailing as a cost saving measure. Why incur the extra expense of having a wireless operator aboard when he would probably be unnecessary? In those dangerously times, most fish and sealing merchants (they were usually one and the same) payed little or no concern when it came to safety issues. As well, often throwing caution to the wind in so doing, being the first sealing vessel to make it back to St John's from the hunt with a full load of pelts, either from "the front" or "the gulf", would be a feather in the owner's cap, and even more so the vessel's skipper. Compounding matters further, for that trip to the ice, Southern Cross also had on board the unusually large number of 173 sealers, all squeezed into overcrowded "living" spaces. But profits came before men's lives in those days.

She was barely discernible through the blizzard when she replied to fellow sealer SS Portia's whistle, with a toot of her own, then just off Cape Pine on the Island's south coast. The Portia's skipper however later noted in his log that the Southern Cross appeared to be lying very low in the water. Neither the Southern Cross nor any of her crew were ever seen or heard from again; nor were any of the sealer's bodies ever recovered.

The SS Newfoundland was an old, "wooden walled" vessel, whose wireless had also been removed, being considered a needless expense. She was then under the command of Wes Kean, son of one of the Island's most renowned and respected sealing captains, Abram Kean who too was at the hunt, in command of Bowring Bros' pride of the sealing fleet, the new ironclad SS Stephano. The elder Kean had already won in 1910, "the high-liner" prize for bringing in the greatest number of pelts from one trip to "the Ice", an impressive 50,000 pelts. Just a few years later he managed to pick up an OBE, (then in his 79th year but still going strong), for bringing in to Bowring Bros. wharf, his one millionth pelt, a truly outstanding lifetime achievement in the sealing business, just the kind of captain you'd want to have on your team.

He had finally located the main herd of seals on that late March morning, and estimated the number to be very large, perhaps two million or more including pups. He informed his son of this by prearranged whistle signal, telling Wes in effect to put his men over the side to commence the hunt. However, as the day wore on, due to very difficult ice conditions over which his men had to cross, Wes could see through his (spy) glass that his men were taking much longer than anticipated to reach the seals, appearing still to be about 2 or 3 miles off. In the event of encountering such problems on the ice, Wes had told his 'master watch', the man in command of the 120 men on the ice, to make for Stephano, which was lying closer to the seal herd than was Newfoundland and spend the night aboard her. Abram somehow either innocently misinterpreted this instruction from Wes or perhaps even chose to ignore it, (this would be very hard to prove during the official enquiry that followed the disaster) and after giving Wes's men a mug up of hot tea and hard tack (sailor's biscuit) he ordered them back on the ice and to return to their own vessel. It was then early in the afternoon. A combination of badly mangled instructions and misinterpreted requests seems to have occurred between the three main players: the father and the son Keans, and the master watch, leading to the calamitous series of events that followed, as later came out in the enquiry.

In the end, the central misunderstanding centered on both captains in assuming the other would be picking up Newfoundland's men later that day. The result being that her crew of 120 sealers, were still out on the ice when the full force of an unexpected spring blizzard swept down upon them later in the afternoon when they were still out on the ice miles from both vessels. Survivors would later testify that they saw Stephano steaming further away from where she had dropped them off earlier in the afternoon, when they began their march back to the Newfoundland.

Out on the ice, a difference in opinion about the course of action to be taken among the men broke out, with most deciding to continue walking back to their own vessel over the rough rafting ice that was by now 7 or 8 miles away. A smaller group headed back for the Stephano, 3 or perhaps 4 miles distant. Within 20 minutes of the blizzard's onset however both vessels became completely lost to view in the blinding snow. Making progress in either direction now became impossible. It was accepted at the inquiry that Capt. Abram was totally unaware that Wes had intended him to keep Wes's crew with him that night, with the result that he made no effort by blowing his whistle and using spot lights to recall the 120 men to his vessel when the storm struck later in the afternoon, the procedure he would normally follow to recall his own sealers back to Stephano in the event of a bad storm bearing down. As it was, by late afternoon his own sealers were already all safely back aboard Stephano. The mix up guaranteed that 120 men would be left out on the ice that night with a blizzard raging all around them.

The younger Keen had instructed the master watch at the start to hunt seals in the area between their vessel and the Stephano, which in the late afternoon gloom was just barely visible on the horizon, as she rose and fell from view, on the swells passing under the ice floes. Of course, Wes thought all was well, assuming that his father would pick up his men later in the afternoon and keep them over night. Both men soon retired for the night as the storm settled in, glad to reach the comfort of their snug warm bunks. Meanwhile, on the ice floes as evening fell and darkness came on, some of the men, seeing that the storm was rapidly morphing into a raging blizzard, began to prepare for the worst by constructing wind breaks from the large slabs of rafted ice that lay about, to shelter behind. Soon all 120 men on the ice would be fighting for their lives, clad as they were in only light clothing, for the day had been warm and pleasant when they had set out in early morning. Now they were facing punishingly strong cold winds in rapidly falling temperatures, and would be apparently left exposed, out on the open ice, overnight.

It was not until over two days later, after the blizzard had blown itself out, that a handful of bedraggled survivors were spotted wandering around in a daze on the ice by lookouts on the Stephano. The end result of the mix up was that 78 of the 120 odd men left out on the ice had frozen to death. It was one of the worst sealing disasters to occur in a century. Coupled with the sinking of the Southern Cross, all told, some 250 sealers were lost in a single day.

Only the luckiest, the hardiest, or perhaps the wiliest survived to tell the tale. And grim, moving tales of survival and death they were, as later came to light; many of the doomed found comfort in group hymn singing while others formed prayer circles for comfort that sprung up during the course of the night. Some would later report that they kept "warm" and thus alive by intermittently jumping around on the ice floes, up and down they say they leapt and skipped about the ice pans, and taking turns pummeling each other when standing still, throughout the long hours of darkness. The most touching scene encountered as later reported by rescuers, was that of the frozen human sculpture of three men still standing together in a tight circle, a father with arms wrapped tightly around two young sons, comforting and protecting each other, all three dying together in an unforgettable act of familial love. Like cord wood, the dead were then collected and stacked on the deck of the Stephano and in this shocking manner were brought into St John's harbour where thousands of citizens lined the docks to bear witness to such an unusual event.

A three man board of inquiry was set up some months later with two finding Abram Kean guilty of a serious lack of judgement and the third declaring it all to be an act of god. No further action was taken against Capt. Kean and the reprimand did little to tarnish his god like image.

A minimal hunt is now carried out only by landsmen and by operators of small craft and in that sense is more like it was done by the original settlers in the years before industrial scale hunting was introduced around 1810. The offshore hunting of adult seals from vessels over 65 ft. in length had been banned in 1987 and the taking of harp seal pups, (whitecoats) earlier still, in 1981.

El Perigrino

I came upon a rainbow where it touched the earth
And climbed it 'cross the sky.
Until it fell to earth again, I trudged on high.
No angels did I find…. I do not lie.
I came upon a waterfall and wore it for a while,
Close to my skin, 'till it released me.
And I could walk again.
They say there is some place at sea,
Where water nymphs are said to be
These Thetises I'd like to see
Although I'm pushin' 83

The following little item was recited for me by Reginald Decker; a fisherman cousin of mine from Joe Batts Arm, a community on Fogo Island's north coast, who learned it from his father Pat around 70 or 75 years ago.

"All men were born equal at first, through this and every nation.
The rich among the poor would be, but for wealth and education.
And who could tell in a hundred years,
The bones of the man that wore the ragged jacket"

(A raggedy jacket is also the name given to a young seal during its period of adolescence between its beautiful whitecoat non-swimming stage and its mature fur coat stage.)

The name Fogo was probably given to the island by Portuguese mariners around 1500. Interestingly, it was also the name given by Portuguese explorers to one of the volcanic islands in the Cabo Verde island chain off West Africa, at around the same time.

Newfoundland's Fogo Island is a 25 by 7 mile island in Notre Dame Bay that was settled by migrant fisherman from England and Ireland in the early 18th century.

The vessels of fishing fleets sailed with crews from the Wexford and Waterford counties of Ireland and Cornish men, from the West Country of England, Cornwall, Devon, Dorset and Somerset. These two groups make up almost entirely the non- aboriginal European ancestors of present day Newfoundlanders. Because of the isolation of most Newfoundland outports (i.e. so called for being outside the main port, St. John's) and with practically no in -migration to the island until recent times to speak of, since the conclusion of the Napoleonic wars, the outports have retained the cultural behaviour and speech patterns of those early settlers. In similar fashion, this goes to explain even the Anglo-Irish accents heard around the capital of St. John's today. Along this part of the Island, i.e. the Avalon Peninsula coast, to areas as far south as Placentia Bay, and known commonly as the "southern shore", the lilting speech of the south east county towns of Waterford and Wexford of Ireland dominate. Just a hundred miles up the coast from St John's however, in Trinity Bay, the accent is entirely different. This is a coastal region in which the local population has retained that of its old Cornish ancestor settlers. Only now, and in all regions the old accents and vocabulary have been significantly added to by a newly created local Newfoundland idiom. The ancestors of many places along the north east coast had arrived from places like Bristol, Plymouth and Poole, in Dorset. Poole was a major centre of the migratory fishery for 200 years, a centre where major factories had to be built in order to supply products for the Grand Banks fishery. The best known item among the products turned out probably being the heavy woolen sweater required by crews of the hundreds of fishing vessels departing from that port for the Grands Banks every year, the well- known Guernsey sweater. One can still see today along the streets of Poole the wealth that was brought back to that city's fish merchants in the form of the many mansions built during the heyday of the migratory fishery in the 18th century. Many 17th and 18th century Bonavista and Trinity Bay settlements became the new world homes of Dorset and Cornwall fishermen. Over the centuries a new vocabulary has also gradually been built up in the old Newfoundland outports.

It's a vocabulary created with special meaning to the people living here and a vocabulary that has been documented in scholarly detail in "The Dictionary of Newfoundland English", for those interested in pursuing the topic further.

My relationship with Fogo Is. Is, while not intimate, familial in nature, an ancestral home land, being the birth place of my maternal grandmother in the 1862. She traveled to St. John's as a young teenager to receive further schooling, living while there with the family of well - to-do first cousins, the Morris's. Mr. Morris was then speaker of the House of Assembly and had also been the founder of the Peoples Party a popular political party of the day. His son, Edward Patrick Morris, (a University of Ottawa law alumnus in 1881) 30 years later in 1907, on becoming the Prime Minister of Newfoundland received the knighthood. He held this position until 1917 when he was invited to join Britain's wartime cabinet under Prime Minister Lloyd George, along with the PMs of the other four white commonwealth countries, at which time he was elevated to the hereditary peerage, Sir Edward becoming the First Lord Baron Morris of St John's Newfoundland and Waterford Ireland. In so doing he became the FIRST Roman Catholic to be so honoured in almost 500 years, and the ONLY Newfoundlander to be EVER so honoured. Lord Morris never returned to live in Newfoundland again, his luxurious home in the St John's western outskirts soon becoming the summer residence of the St John's RC Archbishop. The hereditary peerage was abolished by Tony Blair when he became Prime Minister of the U K in the early 1990s.

There is the bust of another famous Morris family member, Edward Patrick's brother, in Bannerman Park in the city's east end. This Morris, a catholic priest, gave his life while tending to sick orphaned RC boys in an orphanage he had established at Manuals, some 10 miles west of the city, during a cholera epidemic that swept through St. John's at the turn of the 20th century. Along with Fr. Morris, eight of his orphaned boys also died during this plague. Other less well-known brothers of the Morris clan included Francis who became a missionary priest in Haiti where he died, and James, a mining engineer who migrated to Perth Australia where he died without ever returning home again, the 5th and last brother also became a local successful politician, becoming a member of the House of Assembly like his brother and father before him.

Many of my Fogo relatives today, are retired fishermen and sailors, most are residents of Joe Batts Arm, a greatly diminished fishing community on Fogo Island. Several of these retired sailors, also served as boatswains or mates on sealing vessels, owned by the Norwegian/Canadian Karlsen Shipping Company of Halifax, among them, the MV Theron, on which I too spent a couple of voyages as a specimen collector for the Fisheries Research Board of Canada (Arctic Unit) during 1961-1963.

The word Fogo was given to this rocky island by Portuguese navigators who were quite active in Newfoundland waters around 1500. The Portuguese word translates as fire in English and may have been given to the place when the Portuguese chanced to witness what might have been ritual fires set by Newfoundland's first inhabitants the Beothuck, atop Brimstone Head, the striking 300 metre high rocky cliff that overlooks panoramically the ocean on three sides here. Around this same time, other Portuguese navigators also gave the Fogo name, to an island in the Cabo Verde Archipelago that lies several hundred miles off the west coast of Africa.

Here, during the centuries that followed, Cabo Verde became a busy holding place for West African slaves and a major centre for European and American slave traders. In the decades following slavery's abolition, many hundreds of Cabo Verdeans crewed on New England whalers, a trade at which many soon excelled, often rising in the ranks to fill important positions like the highly skilled and valued position of harpooner and some even as mate. By the end of the 19th century, hundreds of Cabo Verdeans had settled, with their families, in the whaling centres of New Bedford and Nantucket Mass. After the demise of this industry, many of their descendants simply moved to Gloucester to continue their lives at sea as trawler fishermen on the Banks. From this long established town in New England both Newfoundland's Fogo Island fishermen and Cape Verdean fishermen now came together to share common cause.

The economy of Newfoundland for over 400 years had been one based almost entirely on cod fishing and this lasted right up until the fishery collapsed in 1992 and the federal government was forced to declare a closure putting 30 to 40 thousand people out of work practically overnight. For most of this 400 year period, only one type of fishing was practiced by the island's inhabitants, the so called in-shore fishery and the method of catching, using mainly hand-lines: either a single line with one or two attached baited hooks, the so called "jigging" or a trawl line, perhaps 100 meters long carrying hundreds of baited hooks. The very efficient US invented cod trap came into wide use during the 1890s. These were also the methods employed by Newfoundland fishermen fishing from schooners on the Grand Banks and on the Labrador shore, where many families from bays along the Island's NE coast, pursued a summer fishery that lasted more or less from April until October. These schooner based operations were usually family enterprises with crews of 5 or 6 men, while the much larger Grand Banks schooners might be crewed by up to a dozen men or more. The largest schooners of Lunenburg NS perhaps 120 feet in length, had crews of 20 men. All Newfoundland fisheries used two- man dories for safety reasons.

By way of comparison, the large three mast barks of the Portuguese White Fleets that fished on the Banks using traditional hook and line methods from the 1930s to the 1960s, employed only single man dories. Living and working conditions for these Portuguese fishermen were generally recognized to be extremely tough, i.e. usually two - man bunks with personal clothing being used as bedding and mattresses and a work day often stretching up to 20 hours in length, to go along with a poor diet and no recreation. Working and general living conditions for fishermen aboard Nova Scotian and Massachusetts schooners were generally much better than on Newfoundland owned and operated vessels.

As mentioned above, the American invented cod trap in the 1890s markedly increased catches of Newfoundland in -shore fishermen with their introduction in the early 20th century and soon became a common sight on the Newfoundland inshore fishery. These traps were set (i.e. generally spoken of as 'fixed gear', as opposed to trawls) just off the shore, to catch migrating cod from the Grand

Banks that come inshore in pursuit of spawning capelin, their favourite food, in June and July. The net consists of several "rooms" that lead the cod deeper and deeper inside until, becoming utterly confused, it can't find its way out again. The first net encountered is like a leader net and is set perpendicular to the shore, where it blocks the progress of the fish swimming along the shoreline gorging of capelin, and leads it into the first room of the trap which in turn leads it deeper into another room, and finally into a third room, deep inside the trap, where the fish becomes quite confused and can't find its way out again.

Things suddenly and dramatically changed for men and fish alike in the 1920s with the arrival of the first modern steam trawlers (draggers) on the scene. Now, quite independent of weather conditions, vessels could scoop up tens of thousands of fish more with their machine controlled trawls than when fishing from wind dependent schooners and in just a fraction of the time. While the inshore fishery had remained local, the off-shore had always been recognised as foreign, and after 1920 more so than ever.

In many respects Newfoundland's life style until the 1950s, had closely resembled that of Iceland's, with one major difference, an absence of good soil for farming in Iceland. But Newfoundland's is only marginally better on the rocky east coast, in addition to there being only a short growing season here. The south west coast has very much better weather and soil for farming but major settlement never took hold there due to its being quite out of the way for newly arriving English and French based fishing crews from Europe. But in one respect, Newfoundland and Iceland were both islands with one single, life sustaining dominate activity, cod fishing. There was one major difference however in that in Iceland fishing was absolutely essential to its very survival. This was not regarded with the same urgency in Newfoundland, especially after confederation with Canada. Similarly, Iceland and Newfoundland had both been the recipients of huge US investment during the 2nd world war that in many ways brought both of them into the modern world. One major difference came about however when Iceland gained independence from Denmark in 1944, when it almost immediately declared a 5-mile territorial fishing limit, which quickly morphed into a 12 mile and then a 50 -mile zone by 1972. Canada on the other hand didn't get into the protective fishing zone game until the 1960s and didn't get around to setting its own tough 200 mile Economic Exclusion Zone (EEZ) until 1977 Iceland, realizing that its very survival depended on the cod fishery determined early on to forcefully protect it and set about doing this with gunboats, thereby triggering a short lived Cod fish war with the main offender, the UK.

Around this same time, Newfoundland's history took a decidedly different tack than Iceland's when it voted in a second referendum to join Canada as its 10th province in 1949. Historically, it had already rejected this option a number of times in the past; wisely realizing that its economy and life style were unique and decidedly unlike Canada's, a large federal system, a country in which it would be swallowed up and soon have little control over its own fishing regulations. But that all changed in 1949, when the electorate by a very slim majority of less than 2 percent, voted to join its larger sister dominion. Before long, its worst fears were realized with regard to the fishery. To many Newfoundlanders, a federal government situated thousands of miles away in Ottawa, knew little about and cared even less about Newfoundland's fishery. (Additionally, soon to arrive on the scene would be the disastrous Labrador hydro -electric power fiasco agreement with Quebec, in which Quebec gets 99% of the profits for 79 years.) Iceland still seems to chart its own course in the 21st century as witness to how it choose to handle the recent economic turmoil of 2008, when it told both the World Bank and IMF to literally get lost rather than follow their dictates, to introduce harsh humiliating austerity measures. Although now representing only 5% of the work force, the fishery is still the major economic driver of the economy. In stark contrast on the other hand, Newfoundland's fishery has been reduced to only a shadow of its former glory when the motto: IN COD WE TRUST actually meant something.

Now there is also wealth coming from recently discovered off-shore oil and gas and the financial returns earned from these resources have had a major impact on the province's economy (just as they have in Norway, another country with which Newfoundland can bear some comparison) and the state has finally had the ability to increase spending on important social services for its citizens. In retrospect, perhaps it has been only too eager and too generous in this regard.

The Spanish Captain

You muses nine may you combine and help me in my song
In sweet refrain or sad lament it won't delay you long.
I left my home in sunny Spain as you may understand
To sail out on a Caravel bound out for the new-founde-land.
In Greenland's Sea, the walrus roar and make an awful din
As smartly cross the ice we skip, right smartly haul them in.
On to the pole our captain cries, if must we'll go again
But catch me now the right whale boys not mike hump or fin.
Now on these grand banks, once full of fish, their ghostly voices sing,
I hear them just beneath the wave, and upon sea gull's wing.

*bowhead and right whales (Greenland) were the commercially hunted 'right' whales of the 19th century in the northern oceans.

M. V. Theron

Arctic research vessel/seal hunter

The M V Theron was built in Greenock on the Clyde, Scotland in 1949, with the additional strong selling points of a reinforced (double) steel hull for working in polar ice conditions and several refrigerated holds. Her envious life history was changed permanently for the worse when she was sold to J. and A. Puddister and Co. of St John's Newfoundland for around $350,000 in 1980 for the very un-glamourous purpose of hauling general cargo around the Island. Until that date she had been the prized jewel in the crown of the Karl Karlsen Shipping

Co (Lines) of Halifax, working almost continuously for thirty years as an arctic research vessel and seasonal sealer for the Karlsen Co under charter to the Canadian government. She built up an interesting profile over that 30 year period, highlighted by her involvement in the V (Bunny) Fuchs and Ed Hillary co-jointly led first successful Commonwealth /UK Trans Antarctic Expedition (TAE) via the south pole in 1955-1958, when Theron was captained by her long time Norwegian/Canadian skipper, Harald Maro of Halifax NS. Theron had been selected to transport and disembark on the Antarctic flow edge (Shackleton Base) the eight man advance party of the expedition and the gear needed to make the expected three year crossing of the continent via the South Pole, from the Weddell Sea to the Ross Sea. Theron was a very handsome vessel visually, both inside and out, with her brilliant white exterior hull and sleek silhouette and interior salons finished with attractive mahogany paneling and brass fittings. She was: 181 ft. in length, with 33 ft. beam and draft of 16 ft. and a weight of 850 tonnes gross. She had been purchased in 1950, only a year after her launch, by the well -known Norwegian fishing/ whaling/sealing company The Karlsens of Olsen, from whence most of the officer crew came, with Harald Maro in command, who remained her first and only captain, for over a 27 year period.

She worked in the Newfoundland sealing industry for many years with intentions at the beginning of also pursuing the whale fishery but by the early years of the 1950s this fishery had already collapsed through over fishing. A long career then began for the vessel supporting scientific research teams in Canada's arctic regions, under contract to the Canadian federal government where she became engaged in the charting and mapping of arctic waters and adjacent shorelines. From the very beginning Karl Karlsen invited aboard and comfortably accommodated government scientific and technical workers (she could squeeze 35 into her smallish accommodations) while they pursued their professional activities. Among this group were also included FRB people, which explains my presence aboard. But her lasting claim to fame truly had arrived when she was chosen to transport the British-Commonwealth Advance Expeditionary Party to the Antarctic continent in 1955 where she safely landed them at Shackleton Base after encountering many difficulties.

The Whalefish

(And sung to the melody to an early 18th century song, The Olde Mole)

We sailed aboard in Theron's crew, in the year of '61,
Put our trust in Maro brave, whose equal there was none.
So outward bound we made away, our homes we left behind,
For the place of icy waters cold, the whalefish there to find.
Caught fast we lay in the arctic sea, that ice we could not flee,
For 50 days and nights we sailed, that mighty fish to see.
At last we spied our mighty prize, he blew a spout so high,
When 'err he blew we heard the cry, go catch him now me byes.
So with our mates we then gave chase, this truth I tell today,
There from the deep and full of fight our mighty whalefish lay.
Our deadly darts we shot away, to hook that blubbered hide,
That mighty fish went straight he down, from fright we nearly died.
He left us there in disarray, our only chance you see,
To cut our lines and leave him there, and set old whalefish free.
A'whalin' I'll not go again, on that you can be sure,
I'll stay on land and take a wife, I'll hunt whalefish no more!

St John's Jail

As sung to The English Huntsuppe an early 18th century melody.

Come all ye lads from far and near,
And a song I'll sing so lend an ear.
About the day my luck did fail,
And land me in a St John's Jail.

(Chorus)

A sailor's plight, confined tonight,
My happy home, Oh! No!
I'll see never more.

I sailed out on the Black Ball Line,
When first I went to sea, me byes.
In prison cast, I'm now caught fast,
A cruel circumstance, you see.

(Chorus)

My prison lies here by the sea,
Its roll on shore my company.
A misadventure, me in tow,
Hard bread cold water, now well I know.

(Chorus)

European Settlement

I didn't know it during the years I was growing up in Newfoundland during the 1940s and 50s, but it was brought to my attention by a professor of Anthropology at Memorial University of Newfoundland, during a radio talk on CBC in which he stated that Newfoundlanders whose ancestors had settled in the White Bay area prior to 1800 CE, most likely had indigenous ancestors and present day relatives. My ears perked up at this announcement, for I had just learned from a family genealogy expert that we had relatives who fit this very criterion. Our 18th century ancestor (1770s) was a man named Reeves, a fish merchant's agent, recently sent to Newfoundland by the company's head office in Poole, Somerset, England to supervise operations on the Island as well as drum up new business. In so doing, he likely became a livyer as well (one who overwintered in Newfoundland).

After overseeing the already successful fishing station on Fogo Island, Notre Dame Bay for a year or two, he expanded the firm's reach by moving north to the newly settled outport of Englee in White Bay. in the mid -1770s. Mr. Reeves' granddaughter was my great grandmother, Margaret Reeves, born c 1830s, mother to my grandmother Ellen Emberly, born 1862 in Joe Batts Arm, Fogo Is.

Poole, along with other English ports on Britain's south west coast, became a busy focal point for recruiting crews and supplying the Grand Banks fishery. As mentioned above the city became famous for manufacturing the heavy woolen sweaters known as Guernseys, a favourite of Banks fishermen. The many 18th and 19th century mansions seen in Poole today stand as reminders of the great profits made from the Grand Banks fishery.

The Decline of King Cod

Statistics gathered by the Dept. of Fisheries and Oceans abounded, but like the warnings of in-shore fishermen during the early 1980s, were ignored.....
Fishermen had begun noticing a major decline in the size of individual fish during that decade (i.e. older fish, were once found as large as 6 or 7 feet in length, and now were rarely seen to be more than two or three feet in length). Old female cod, by far the most fecund and prolific of the species, with annual egg production as high as nine million eggs, were simply not showing up in the catches any more. Egg counts now of only hundreds of thousands of eggs, as produced by much younger immature females, were being seen.

Sealers may have continued to take upwards of 500, 000 seals in the hay day years of sealing in the 1840s and 1850s. But cod fishermen on the Banks were certainly not taking catches off the Gran Banks in the 1980s any longer like the 810,000 tonnes taken in the record year of 1968. Catches its true had been building year over year after giant sized factory trawlers began showing up in ever increasing numbers on the Banks in the mid- 1950s, with each trawler now catching as much fish in an hour as a local fishing schooner took off the Banks in an entire season. A sustainable fishery in 1968 is estimated by fishery scientists was put at best at being in the 250,000 tonne range. A catch of 810,000 tonnes that year could only predict a disaster lay ahead for the fishery which in fact did occur in 1992. Fish simply could no longer be found in numbers anymore.

Population loss in Newfoundland

Since 1992 out migration from the Island has been 50,000 plus, the number of fishermen and allied fish workers thrown out of work almost overnight with the fishery closure. Astonishingly, the birth rate in Newfoundland had fallen in a decade from being the highest in Canada to being the lowest. Social problems have accompanied the cod collapse in the form of family breakdown and alcoholism. Until very recently, it was the only province in Canada with a net decrease in population. In especially hard hit localities, fisheries of other underutilized species and aquaculture have started up, some with very impressive results: species like sea urchins, as well as cold water snow crab and shrimp now comprise the catch. However, the Island's debt is soaring again, the major problem being demographic in nature. The place now simply has too few working young people to pay for the many medical bills of the (too many) old.

War Time St John's

Because of the successful activities of German subs in nearby Conception Bay, with the sinking of several iron ore carriers in 1942, a heavy antisubmarine net was strung across the entrance to St. John's harbor to protect vessels there from torpedo attack. The net was placed at the entrance's narrowest point, known as "the Narrows", a point not much more than 50 meters across. A couple of times torpedoes were later launched from submarines against vessels in the naturally shielded harbour but detonated harmlessly on striking either the net or protective rocks around the entrance to the harbour. With this net in place, shipping within the harbor, and most importantly the escort vessels of the North Atlantic Squadron, were made safe from sub attack.

My father, like most men not serving in the military during the war, had been 'drafted' into the local ARPs (Air Raid Patrol). Their duties were, in addition to putting out fires caused by incendiary bombs should that scenario ever arise, and enforcing the lights out regulations in the city after sundown. The ARPs while walking the streets after dark made sure that window blinds were completely pulled down so that no light could be seen from the outside. The shrouded city, drawn down like this as darkness fell, descended into a spooky kind of demi world during the war years. Adding to the spooky atmosphere, automobiles had their headlights also fitted with black metal hoods (bonnets) that kept the light directed down onto the roadway, allowing little light to escape skyward, something that could alert any enemy aircraft flying overhead. To help prevent accidents on such a shadowy stage, the lower few feet of telephone poles and roadside tree trunks were white washed.

For years after war's end I remember playing with my father's WW2 issued gear, items like an old WW1 type gas mask and standard issue military helmet. Along with these there were also a 2 gallon aluminum water bucket kept full of sand and a small hand operated water pump, for extinguishing the incendiary fires. To my knowledge my dad was never called upon to use any of this fire extinguishing equipment although I do remember him suiting up when on duty to make his nightly ARP rounds. To complete the image of protector/policeman and give themselves some authority, the ARPs wore in addition a wide arm band with the initials ARP clearly emblazoned on it.

Newfoundland was once again in 1939, a British colony, having been compelled to surrender its Responsible Govt status (the first and only time this had been done, although in so doing it never lost its dominion status) and return in beggar's garb, to Great Britain for rescue in 1933, during the height of the great depression.

At the height of the depression because of mounting debt, Newfoundland found itself unable to pay its bills and was indeed on the brink of declaring bankruptcy when it sought to be taken back again by Britain with a status somewhere twixt colony and dominion.

This sad state of affairs had many causes including local political greed and corruption. However, it must also be noted that Newfoundland had been left in this economic straight jacket partly because of the huge interest free loan she had foolishly given Britain during WW1, a loan that most knowledgeable economists at the time fully realized could never be paid off. Not only was there this enormous monetary debt hanging over it in 1933, but Newfoundland had also lost greatly in human terms in the Great War, in that she had lost the finest of an entire generation of her young men in the war. Especially catastrophic was the grievous loss suffered at Beaumont Hamel (Battle of the Somme) in 1916 when practically the entire Newfoundland Regiment of approximately 808 men was wiped out; leading it to be awarded the honorarium 'Royal' shortly afterwards.

Confederation with Canada

In 1949, almost an entire century of responsible self–government, first won in 1855 ended, with the exception of the period between 1933 and 1949 when the Island was governed by a British Commission comprising of six commissioners, three local appointees and three British appointees, and an overseeing British Governor. Scant improvement was seen economically under the Commission of Government, and with the exception of the tireless work undertaken by one British commissioner, Mr. Hope Simpson, little of value was seen to be done in the reluctant colony. Thanks to Hope Simpson however, for the very first time on the Island and in Labrador social and medical services were set up at the government level. In recognition and as a reward, he is remembered today by the Labrador town named after him, Port Hope Simpson. Along the Labrador coast and in northern Newfoundland such things had long been neglected if not totally ignored, by successive government politicians in St. John's, who had cheerfully let education and medical services be looked after by the Moravian Missionaries in Labrador, (who were doing just that since the 1760s), and the Grenfell International Association, the chief health care provider to Northern Newfoundlanders and Labradoreans since being set up by Dr. Wilfred Grenfell in the 1890s. Why should politicians bother with such things when they were already being attended to by others, they reasoned? This laissez-faire attitude continued until confederation with Canada in 1949.

New Wealth and Status

(Construction of WW2 US Military Bases Brings Wealth, Vigour and Renewed Dignity to the Island).

With the entry of the USA into the war things became strikingly better economically in Newfoundland almost overnight. For the first time in many decades (and possibly for many the very first time ever), such prosperity had not been witnessed on the island, most of it due to major construction projects that got under way almost immediately after the entry of the US into the war. There was practically a friendly invasion of the Island by the US military early in 1942. The happy sounds of hammers hitting nails and saws cutting boards, could be heard all the way from St John's to Goose Bay in Labrador and several points between.

But following war's end talk soon came around to the political future of the Island again. After several years of discussions involving Canada, the UK and Newfoundland it was decided that its future would be decided by referenda. The first offered the three following choices:

1) Confederation with Canada,
2) Responsible Government as before 1933
3) Economic Union with the USA, a surprise offering that had sprung up late due to some mild interest having been shown in the US Congress.

A continuation of the Commission of government that had existed since 1933 however was not on the table. Britain definitely wanted out.

In this first referendum, Economic Union with the US came last, getting only 15 % of the vote and was by mutual agreement dropped from the next referendum.

In the second, held in 1948, the showdown was a hardly fought duel between confederate and anti- confederate forces. Interestingly, the 15% of the population that was now up for grabs, gave the confederates the victory, when they collected 10% of that vote, leaving the anti-confederates with only 5%.

In this final referendum Newfoundland had opted to join Canada, by a narrow margin. (Roughly 51% vs. 49%). In these referenda, a wide divide had become obvious between the citizens of St. John's, (including the Avalon area in general), where the vote strongly supported responsible government, and the outports, where the population voted overwhelmingly for confederation with Canada. It is agreed that the confederates won the day thanks to the very persuasive oratorical skills of Joe Smallwood, their leader, (soon to become the province's first premier), who working tirelessly, and with few lieutenants, cleverly played on the outport family's typical lack of cash, due to the medieval fish trade's Truck System, persuaded it with lures of Canada's riches, riches that could be theirs simply by voting YES! Hard cash programmes like family allowance, the baby bonus, and unemployment insurance lay in Ottawa waiting for the taking. With confederation, real hard cash would be put into the pockets of all the people, many for the first time, some whom had ever seen hard cash before.

When the shocking results of the referendum were announced on March 31, 1949, (ironically the eve of April Fool's Day), I remember the citizenry of St. John's strapping on black arm bands and drawing down their window blinds for several days, to show their anger, sadness, disappointment and frustration to all who would record this incomprehensible event.

Patriotism

St. John's kids don't need no sleds, they slide down hills on cod fish heads…………………………..

Though Newfoundland is changing fast

Some things we must not lose.

May we always have our flipper pies

And CODFISH for our brewis. (from a 19th century sealer's song)

The following inscription was discovered on an outhouse door somewhere on the northeast coast.

The codfish lays 10,000 eggs,

The hen she lays but one.

The codfish she makes ne'er a sound,

The hen cackles when she's done.

Now the lowly cod she gets no praise,

But our hen, she's such a prize,

Which only goes to show ya,

That it pays to advertise.

Certain imagines from boyhood are still clearly remembered viz. the ubiquitous coal cinders lying about on our steep hilly streets and sidewalks in wintertime to help get our around safely without breaking an arm or leg.

Negotiating these sidewalks would sometimes be near impossible, without the welcome sight of an available bucket of coal cinders nearby, left outside the city's houses for collection or perhaps just for such an emergency. Frequently, as an act of kindness, or to assist visitors to the premises the home owners often threw a shovel full or two of ashes in front of their houses; whatever, they were usually there awaiting use by the stranded or fearful passerby. The savings to provincial health care bills for broken bones must have been greatly reduced thanks to the coal cinders.

For the motorist, coal cinders were almost as essential as a set of chains for navigating the city's wintertime hilly streets and drivers could constantly be seen scampering around from vehicle to sidewalk in search of a bucket of these life savers. Racing back to their machines with the valuable cargo they'd spread it skillfully around the auto's rear wheels for traction and soon make a clean getaway either home or on to make the next delivery if a delivery van. Even vehicles equipped with chains could at times be left helpless if not for the availability of coal cinders left outside homes on the sidewalks. One constant downside however to burning coal, in addition to others more serious, was the constant need to clear soot and cinders out of our eyes, whenever walking outside in wintertime, an irritant that often required the assistance of a fellow pedestrian to successfully remove with the help of a hankie or tissue.

St. John's harbour is rather small, not much more than a mile or so in length and less than half that in width, so the doubling up or even tripling up of vessels at harbour side wharves became a common sight at times. This was most apparent in modern times when the Portuguese White Fleet was still fishing on the Grand Banks between 1933 and 1974 and during WW2, when many corvettes might be in port at the same time. St John's by 1942 had become an important hub for RCN escort vessels on UK bound North Atlantic convoys loaded with war material and cargoes of food that had formed up in Bedford Basin Halifax. This daring little fleet of small corvettes and frigates became immortalized in the North Atlantic Squadron song that was frequently heard sung during the war and in the years immediately after. The naval officers club in St John's was The Crow's Nest, the entrance to which was situated at the top of a 30 ft. long outside fire escape accessed at the side of a building on the east side of the War Memorial on Duckworth St. Our house at the bottom of Victoria St was less than a 10 minute walk to both the Crow's Nest and the harbour's wharves so we became rather expert at most things naval and harbour activities in general during the war. During these years, coordinating the movement of so many vessels in such a small space at any one time was something of a nightmare, yet there were no major collisions in the harbour during WW2. Probably the most congested spot of all was at the head of the harbour, where broken down or damaged vessels queued up, awaiting their turn for repairs in the city's rather limited dry dock facility.

Within a decade after war's end there was another noticeable change in the harbour's occupants even as things returned to 'normal'. Technical advances made during WW2 greatly contributed to the modernization of fishing fleets. By the mid -1950s the noble fishing schooner of old had all but disappeared, and its place taken by the modern highly mechanized trawler that was soon to wreck the fishing industry entirely. Within a twenty year period of modern intensive fishing the fish were left with no place to hide thereby spelling their near disappearance from the area.

Early Employment at FRB

I first went to work for the Fisheries Research Board of Canada in the early 1950s, finding employment at their St John's station following my freshman year at MUN. I began my career as an assistant specimen collector and lab technician and remained performing these duties during summer holidays while a student at MUN.

The first specimens I collected for the FRB were otoliths from Redfish (Rosefish), caught on the Grand Banks by Spanish trawlers. After collecting my redfish samples from the trawlers I returned to our lab to dissect out the animal's otoliths, tiny cartilaginous ear organs that contribute to fish stability and balance in the water column while swimming in the ocean. Thin slices were first shaved off these samples that were then lathed down even further, so that eventually the number of concentric rings they contained could be counted, (like those on a tree trunk) with a binocular microscope; with each ring understood to represent one year's growth. During this early redfish phase of my career I was supervised by an attractive, blond, thirtyish Basque Spaniard, Dr. Alfonso Rojo, who was spending a year at the St John's FRB station because of the abundance of redfish available here for his research. He had arranged before arriving to work at the station to have samples collected from the numerous Spanish trawlers that visited St John's regularly for bait, supplies and repairs. The FRB St John's station had a cute little 55 ft. recently built schooner that was used for making only short local cruises around neighbouring bays where staff collected samples from the water column by towing small non-commercial size trawls behind. Only rarely were voyages ventured out to the Banks from Burin on the south coast of the Island. From my lab window perch I often sat boringly counting the rings on my redfish samples gazing down to where this little vessel lay at anchor, looking almost toy like, just off our private wharf, looking so gay and spritely with her pennant flying in the breeze, in her fresh spring coat of bright green paint and scrubbed clean decks. She had been christened with the catchy name 'Canalus', a commonly occurring, free swimming, tiny ocean crustacean, and a major food source for many animals in the food chain, ranging from baleen whales to tiny fishes like capelin.

For my second and third summers at the station, I had a new boss, a mildly eccentric Englishman, named Dr. David Sergeant. He turned out to be a recently minted PhD from Cambridge and a man who was to turn up again at a later stage in my FRB career. (He became my boss again almost 10 years later at the FRB's (Arctic Unit) in Montreal, where he was doing beluga whale and harp seal research). Upon first arriving at the St John's station his desire had been to do research solely on harp seals but the station director Dr. Wilfred Templeton had cajoled him into undertaking the study of long fin pilot whales. A conveniently large population of these animals was always close at hand, only a hundred or so miles to the north, in Dildo Trinity Bay, where they were driven ashore and slaughtered annually during the 'pot-head' whale drive.

From what I gathered, this drive seemed to be a variant of the rambunctious 'hunt' that was still going on in the Faroe Islands. As described there, the hunt gets under way with local fishermen sailing out to nearby waters where large pods of these whales have recently been spotted, where the men then create a racket by banging on pots and pans and the like. This ruckus understandably causes panic among the large whale pods, ultimately resulting in a mass stranding, at which time the slaughtering takes place. The Dildo hunt, in many ways seems to be very similar. During the 1950s, Dildo's pilot whales were still being driven ashore and slaughtered for their oil and for use as food on local fox farms. The fox farms may have been a make work programme set up by the premier.

Again, as with my work on redfish the previous summer, I underwent a brief period of training. The work this time involved the extracting of canine teeth from long fin pilot whales, a task somewhat more difficult than had been the removing of otoliths from redfish that I'd done during the previous year.

I drove off to Dildo in the Station's pickup truck with my dental tools, glycerine tubes, glass bottles, tubs, and crates piled in the back early the following week, in time to catch the drive then already under way.

The fishermen here first run the whale pods into shallow waters around the cove where they can easily be got at and dispatched with harpoons, knives, and guns. Luckily, I escaped much of the slaughter that had occurred during the morning drive by arranging my arrival for early afternoon.

During the next few hours I was kept busy extracting teeth and filling vials with stomach contents and jars with reproductive organs collected from the scores of dead animals lying about.

The methodology for aging these whales proceeds along lines like that for the redfish: slicing very thin strips of tissue from the teeth and grinding them down so that the rings can be easily counted under the binocular microscope. Again, each ring represents one year's growth of tissue in the tooth.

These panicked whale strandings seem quite similar to what occurs at times in nature, where they also occur for unexplained reasons or for no apparent reason. After listening to whale chatter on repeated recordings some authorities speculate that it's possible an entire family unit or even the entire pod, may become stranded while seemingly responding to the distressed call of just a single animal, perhaps a matriarchal figure. In so doing, perhaps they are responding to some innate urge to offer comfort or aid of some kind to such an individual. In this scenario it could be that an entire chain reaction of mass strandings may be triggered by the vocal clicks of just this one single individual (or perhaps a pair of animals), that have become trapped on shore simply by misjudging an outgoing tide while pursuing food. Navigation errors could also be contributing factors in tricky shallow waters often seen along crescent shaped tidal beaches or points of land that extend into the sea as have been recorded in New Zealand's south island.

It's unknown why certain whale species more than others tend to behave in this way, although a number of theories have been put forward, chief among them the increased sociability of these stranding whales. The most vulnerable to exhibitions of this macabre behaviour seem to be pilot whales and their close cousins, the orcas, both medium sized 20-25 ft. toothed whales. [Note: In Newfoundland and many other places, pilot whales are commonly called pot heads because of the distinctive shape of their heads. This tendency to strand is obviously being exploited at Dildo during their annual "drives".]

In the 19th century, these medium sized toothed whales were usually called blackfish by New England whalers, although generally not hunted, being considered too small to be worth the effort. Many outward bound whalers though did hunt blackfish, perhaps to give inexperienced new crew some practice in hunting whales from whaleboats, in the absence of larger trophies to catch.

Almost immediately following my resignation from FRB to pursue a PhD, several interesting job offers came my way, from both academia and within the whaling industry itself. This was still almost a decade before industrial whaling was banned in 1974 and "great" whales like the Sperm and the Blue were still being routinely hunted although they were becoming quite scarce. The International Whaling Commission was still the overseer of ruling the industry (for better or for worse) at the time and it was through them that my industry employment offers came. Two of these enquiries arrived from the most active participants still in the business, Japan and Norway. They still remain so today, 5 decades on, along with Iceland. In an attempt to lessen its perceived guilt in the eyes of the world and perhaps to ward off criticism, Japan claims to be hunting whales solely for scientific purposes. But there are very strong cultural factors at play here as well, for whale meat is still widely eaten in Japan.

My job offers however would involve my being at sea for very long stretches of time, stationed aboard deep ocean whalers for months on end. Both appealed to my sense of adventure and in the case of Norway, there was the added lure of possibly renewing old acquaintances. I decided to sit on the offers for a while before jumping in, as neither needed an urgent reply.

The duties involved for both positions seemed rather minimal, basically not much more than keeping records of whale sightings and captures, the species involved and the exact positions sighted and captured. The Japanese fleet would be remaining in the Southern Ocean for the duration of their voyages including sorties into Antarctica. The Norwegian vessels intended to restrict their activities to the Atlantic and Arctic Oceans.

Another interesting offer came from a well- funded US research outfit, the Cetacean Research Laboratory in Torrance California. For the most part it was land based field work but would involve frequent traveling along the state's coast with an all-terrain vehicle.

To help me select one of these three offers I revisited Herman Melville's 1851 fictionalized memoir Moby Dick for inspiration, as well as the highly regarded true account of late 19th century whaling by Frank Bullen: The Cruise of the Cachalot (published in 1898). Melville was a middle class youth more city bred than farm boy, who, seeking adventure like many other young men of the day, signed on as ordinary seaman aboard a New England whaler, after only one year's experience at sea working aboard a North Atlantic trader, on the New York to Liverpool run. After perhaps only five years at sea, with the final stint a year in the US Navy, Melville retired to what was at first a very promising writing career of exotica travel, recounting exciting tales about his adventures in the South Pacific. At the same time he also attempted to launch a career as a public speaker, something at which he was not very successful however, due to an uninspiring delivery style. In these endeavours he laboured for a further 5 years before packing- it -in and marrying "UP" as they say, the daughter of a wealthy important N Y state official, and eventually settling in as a middling customs and excise officer in NYC.

English born Bullen on the other hand had been at sea almost from childhood having been taken as a seven year old to be cabin boy aboard an uncle's North

Atlantic trader. Over time he worked his way up the ladder to become first mate, a highly skilled position, on board New England whalers in the 1870s. He too retired to a land lubber job in his late middle age, taking a job in the harbour pilot's office.

Bullen remarkably, for a full time sailor, was a very religious man in both word and deed, with a copy of the bible always close at hand. He remained committed throughout his lifetime to bettering the lot of seamen ashore, similar in nature to other Seamen's Missions of the day. He remained deeply troubled throughout his life by the lack of alternative "healthy" activities for seaman to occupy their time ashore after voyages, and set himself to organizing things for them to become engaged in like picnics into the countryside and the like. Such entertainments seem perhaps more like diversions, activities contrived to keep seamen out of the rough and tumble dock side rum shops and brothels that encircled every harbour at the time and the usual places in which they usually gathered following voyages.

Something caught my eye during these re-readings that I hadn't particularly noticed on first reading; namely, how varied the makeup of the crews was aboard these New England whalers, with non -Americans often outnumbering the native born. Not only that, but also that they frequently occupied important specialized positions aboard ship. Many in these whaling crews were so-called "Portugueseas", highly experienced whale men recruited from the Azores and the Cape Verde Islands off West Africa. Many others came aboard initially as overly eager volunteers from the South Pacific islands frequently visited by these ships and were often taken on as the need arose, which was often, due to the numerous desertions encountered as the voyage progressed. (The imagined glamourous and adventurous aspects of this life seldom matched reality, and seldom lasted longer than a few months as Melville himself discovered). Frequently these foreigners rose to important positions on the whaling ship, like harpooner, as we see on the Pequot, or even a 4th mate as on the Cachalot in Bullen's memoir.

The awareness of the Portuguese to the citizens of St John's was quite strong due to the annual visits for bait, resupplying and repairs of that country's White Fleet while fishing on the Grand Banks for six months of the year. I had also read in Newfoundland Labrador history about the strong contributions of Portugal to the early exploration of the area around 1500 CE. Additionally, it's been more recently confirmed that there was a substantial Portuguese whaling station operating seasonally, roughly from 1510 to 1590, on the Strait of Belle Isle Labrador coast, at present day Red Bay. The station was finally abandoned it is suspected, because of over fishing of the area's local population of Bowhead and Right Whales.

Of particular personal interest, is the case of Fogo Island in Notre Dame Bay Newfoundland, so named by one of the early Portuguese explorers, whoever that may have been and the coexistence of another Fogo Island in the Cape Verde Island archipelago chain off Africa's west -coast. The word itself simply means "fire", but what could be the connection between the identical naming of the two? Were there native peoples on both these islands at the time lighting bonfires atop their mountains?

The year 1949 was one of huge import locally due to a complete change in Newfoundland's political identity. It was the year the Island's 550,000 people decided in two referenda in 1947 and 1949, to join Canada and become its 10th province. As anticipated, it was a very divisive and nasty fight resulting in a division of the population into two almost equal halves, often based on religion, culture and geography. The capital's (St. John's) population and most of the surrounding RC area of the Avalon, were predominately anti-confederate, while their confederate opponents (mostly Protestant), held the rest of the island i.e. most of the outport population. The anti-confederates were voting for a return to responsible government, the political system that had governed the island continuously from 1854 until 1933, when, during the height of the depression the Island fell into near bankruptcy and was forced to return to near colonial status when a British administered Commission Government was installed. Yet, even then, Newfoundland continued to hold on to its status as a Dominion during that 14 year orphan period between 1933 and 1949. The pro-confederates, scattered throughout the island's many coves and bays, had been understandably seduced by Mr. Smallwood, confederation's seductive spokesman and the promise that real hard cash (for many a first time experience, among the Island's fishing families) would become available to them after confederation by way of Canada's social programmes: family allowance, (the baby bonus) and unemployment insurance. These promised rewards swung a very close vote in favour of the confederates. In St. John's however, following the announcement of the results on March 31, 1949, the citizens of St. John's drew down their window blinds and donned black arm bands, overcome by sadness and anger. It had been the cruelest of April fool's jokes to play on the city. Their side had lost by a mere 2 %, with only 51.5 % voting in favour of confederation. A 400 year- old separate identity for an Island's identity thus came to an end overnight.

Early Days of Europeans in Newfoundland Labrador

Newfoundland's Irish immigrants must not be confused with the one million Irish that fled their country to settle in the United States and Canada at the time of the potato blight famine in the 1840s. Indeed there has been little in-migration of any kind to Newfoundland after about 1820, the last large batch arriving at the close of the Napoleonic Wars.

Newfoundland's first "permanent" European settlers, starting as far back as the late 16th century were illegals. [Note: Only three Royal charters for settlement had been awarded over almost a two hundred year period, the most well -known being that of Lord Baltimore's at Ferryland on the Irish Shore in the early 1600s. It failed due to the harsh winter conditions and moved to the USA where it founded Baltimore Maryland.] This odd 'illegal' state of affairs existed until the early 18th century, the result of laws passed in the English Parliament prohibiting the building of any permanent structure on the Island within 2 miles of the coast. Influential parliamentarians representing wealthy West Country fish merchants in Devon, Dorset and Somerset who had controlled fishing operations on the Grand Banks and in areas around Newfoundland's North East coast from the very beginning, saw to it that there would be no competition allowed to take hold on the Island. In this way, these merchants maintained in effect a monopoly on the fishery for upwards to nearly three hundred years, until the American Revolutionary War broke the monopoly and English fish merchants began to be undersold by American and French merchants, who began selling better and cheaper product into the lucrative Portuguese and Spanish markets that had been the private domain of the English for so long.

Newfoundland's first permanent European settlers were most likely solitary fishermen from English vessels on the Grand Banks and the fishing grounds around the Avalon. The Banks fishery was an annual seasonal one, with sailings out to the fishing grounds in the spring and a return back home in the fall. In time, tired of making these yearly transatlantic crossings, more and more of the fishermen understandably elected to try overwintering in Newfoundland, regardless of the tough winter conditions encountered there. They rightly began to ask, why bother with the additional hardships, dangers and inconvenience involved in making two dangerous crossings of the Atlantic Ocean yearly when they could over winter in NFLD?

By the late 17th century, crews also begun to be recruited in the Irish ports of Waterford and Wexford, as these were the final ports of call made by outward bound fishing vessels from Devon, Bristol and Poole. The English vessels began to stop here for final water supplies, salt pork and hard bread before crossing over to the Grand Banks. Women, as might be expected, were a scarce commodity on the island for a great many years, but in time more and more began to arrive and then stay, finding that a better life could be had even out here than the one they'd leave behind. These early 17th and 18th century overwintering fishermen and their families in time began to be called "livyers", forging an early entry into the "Dictionary of Newfoundland English".

The law prohibiting the building of permanent structures on the Island within 2 miles of the coast was originally intended to be enforced by Fishing Admirals, who were generally the first fishing captains to arrive on station in the spring. This law proved well- neigh impossible to enforce of course due to Newfoundland's hugely inundated coastline stretching as it does for thousands of miles, providing countess hiding places for solitary fishermen or small clusters of fishermen to set up shop far from the prying eyes of Fishing Admirals.

Realizing such a law was ridiculous being in effect unenforceable, it was in time ignored entirely. But in this way, the ubiquitous Newfoundland outport came into existence, with its salt box style houses, and fishing rooms and stages sitting atop pylons set up among the rocks on the shoreline. Perhaps at the beginning they had indeed sought out secluded and isolated coves around the coast in which to fish, far from the Admirals' fishing grounds, but by the early- 18th century the outport had clearly come into permanent existence and could be found in almost every cove and harbour around the Island. Except on the west coast of the Island, where a major cod fishery never really took hold and remained ignored for settlement by England's West Country merchants due to the added distance involved getting to and from major fish stocks, home ports and European markets

[NOTE: Research done at MUN in St John's, as well as at U of M in Montreal over the past two or three decades has uncovered powerful evidence overturning previously held beliefs that Newfoundland had been only sparsely settled by Europeans during the 16th and 17th centuries due to the harsh laws enacted by English parliaments prohibiting settlement within 2 miles of the coast*. The common wisdom has been that only formal type plantations such as those at Ferryland, Cupids and Placentia were permitted. Nor indeed was Newfoundland the wild unsettled place as portrayed in most early accounts of the place. It is now estimated that as many as 2000 people were already settled on the English Shore alone, with more than this number settled in French areas, i.e. mainly at Placentia by the end of the 17th century. These numbers would compare quite favourably with settlement in other North American areas at the time, like Acadia and the American colonies. This evidence would seem to make sense coupled with the absurdity of trying to enforce the restriction on settlement within 2 miles of the coast by the Fishing Admirals, due to the Island's impossibly long coastline.

*Fishermen of course needed always to be at or near the coast and the fishing grounds, not only to catch fish but also to places with easily accessible space on which to cure (dress) fish.

Norsemen in Newfoundland

It was not cod fishing and whale hunting that brought the first European visitors to Newfoundland though. We now know that the Norseman Leif Erickson, son of Eric the Red, arrived here from Greenland around 1000 AD, probably on a scouting mission for timber with which to build houses and ships back in tree challenged Greenland. There is also a possibility that they were simply looking for a new place in which to settle, or possibly even on a voyage of discovery.

in 1961 Norwegian archeologists, following a hunch, discovered the location of this small but short lived settlement, at present day L'Anse aux Meadows, situated on the very northern tip of Newfoundland, where perhaps as many as 100 Norse once lived for as long as 10 years. The odd present day Newfoundland settlement name contains an awkward contraction of the French word meduse, (jelly fish) that became distorted by local English fishermen over the years from the original L'Anse aux meduse, (Jelly fish Bay) into L'Anse aux Meadows. Such contractions are common in Newfoundland, the most well- known probably being Baie d'Espoir, (Bay of Hope) pronounced by all Newfoundlanders, Bay Despair, the very opposite of its original meaning. Such is the contrary nature of the place.

Who knows why this Norse settlement in the end failed? The most likely explanation being probably ongoing hostilities with local aboriginal peoples, either Beothuk, Innu or even Inuit. (The Norsemen in time also vacated their settlements in Greenland, most likely also because of on-going struggles with Inuit). At L'Anse aux Meadows, the Norsemen apparently traded with native people, using cow's milk as their main item for trade in these exchanges but they drew the line at trading their weapons.

This L'Anse aux Meadows Norse settlement has been imaginatively recreated consisting of several sod covered stone built longhouses and even includes the replica of a small smithy used by the Norsemen for boat and other repairs.

A number of small Norse artifacts in the way of broaches and pins have also been recovered and are now on display along with other items, in a visitor's museum located at the site. It is thought that this particular site was chosen by the Norsemen because of the presence of a suitable beach on which they could haul up and make repairs to their knarrar, a sort of low tech Norse dry dock. The knarrar was a shorter and wider version of the more famous and feared Viking long ship, normally used for raiding. The knarrar was the vessel developed over the years for transporting dry goods, livestock and people between Norse North Atlantic settlements in Norway, the Shetlands, the Faroes, Iceland, Greenland and finally L'Anse aux Meadows. The Inuit had also developed a similar type of craft in the Umiak, a wide flat -bottomed, forty ft. boat for transporting goods and people, designed so that they could pull it right up on the shore above the water line; in addition, the Umiak was also used for hunting Bow Head and Right whales since it offered excellent stability and allowed space for 5 or 6 hunters, the number needed to successfully hunt these animals.

The 1000 AD Viking location at L'Anse aux Meadows and the nearby 1500 AD Basques whaling station, discovered just 2 decades after the Norse discovery by an amateur archeologist, and located just across the Strait of Belle Isle at Red Bay, on the Labrador coast, are now both easily accessible if one doesn't mind the long drive from airports at either Deer Lake or St. John's. From the latter the drive takes about 11 hours to complete but there's lots to see along the way north. The Red Bay site can also be reached from the Quebec side of the Strait entirely by road, as well as by boat. Both the 500th 'discovery' anniversary year of Newfoundland by Cabot in 1497 CE and the 1000th anniversary year of the Norse arrival in Newfoundland in 997 CE were celebrated in 1997 in Newfoundland, with provincially sponsored replica sailings made from Europe of Cabot's Mathew, from Bristol U.K., to Cape Bonavista and a Viking facsimile long ship sailing from Norway to the L'Anse aux Meadow site.

Note: See elsewhere in this book the interesting story behind the discovery of the Basques whaling station at Red Bay, now a UN World Heritage Site as is L'Anse aux Meadows.

A number of European powers had become interested in Newfoundland and its rich bounty of off shore fish since its 'discovery' by Cabot in 1497 CE. As well as the late 15th century arrivals of the Basques who initially came to the Strait of Bell Isle to hunt Right and Bowhead Whales, there were also English, French, and Portuguese, all of whom had come for the cod. All had continued to use traditional methods of hand lines and trawls with baited hooks for fishing over the centuries, so that it had remained a sustainable fishery for 500 years until the 1950s, when catches first became unsustainable.

[Note: Only the Portuguese had continued to employ traditional methods in their Grand Banks fishery (using St. John's acting as a hub for bait, repair and resupply) right up to 1974, when Canada introduced its 200 mile Exclusive Economic Zone (EEZ) thereby putting the Portuguese White Fleet, the least damaging of all international fishing fleets, out of business.]

It is estimated that the total tonnage of cod taken off the Grand Banks over the four hundred year period, roughly from 1520 up to WW2, with all vessels using traditional methods of single man dories and hand lines, was LESS than has been taken 'off' the Banks over the period 1945 -1990, by large modern factory freezer trawlers. These newcomers have included Russia, Germany, China, Korea and many others....

[NOTE: It may be interesting to note that my ancestor (first cousin thrice removed, Sir Edward Patrick Morris, and later First Lord [Baronet] Morris of Waterford), when Prime Minister of Newfoundland in 1910 was perhaps one of the very earliest Americans to sound the alarm with regard to overfishing on the Grand Banks, to wit:

"..... His administration shared the colony's growing concern about fish stocks and safety issues when French steam trawlers began to arrive on the offshore banks in 1910"......... Other notable issues he pressed while at the Imperial Defence Conference in1909 were his suggestions that Newfoundlanders could crew the British navy's new Dreadnoughts and that the British navy might undertake to use Newfoundland cod fish as a staple aboard all its warships. In these latter endeavours however he was only partially successful."

Following his departure for Britain in 1917, where he became a member of Lloyd George's War Cabinet and sat in the House of Lords, he gave up in addition to a large lucrative law practice and rewarding political life, his manorial Beaconsfield residence with its impressive grounds situated in the western outskirts of St. John's on Topsail Rd. After his departure this property was then taken up as the summer residence of the Catholic Archbishop of St. John's, and almost immediately became the permanent residence of His Grace. Lord Morris never returned to live in Newfoundland again, remaining in London until his death at his seat, 8 Louis, off Grosvenor Square London in 1935.]

The Grand Banks Fishery in the 1960s

By the 1960s all the European and Asian fishing fleets were bringing to the Banks giant technically advanced refrigerator factory ships with huge catch capabilities. By using highly mechanized machinery to operate huge nets with mouths of enormous width and employing the latest hi-tech gadgetry in the way of sonar, radar, fish finders and rock-jumper equipped nets, the so called rock hoppers, within a 30 year period they'd effectively emptied the Grand Banks of its fish. Gill netters, now operating in most oceans, using nets of enormous lengths, are now similarly hollowing out the oceans' fish stocks in the upper water column.

Following the introduction of its own EEZ in 1974, to its everlasting shame, Canada having driven the huge foreign trawlers from its areas of jurisdiction on the Banks, leapt eagerly into the void created, filling it with its own huge modern refrigerated trawlers. The overfishing simply continued as before.

The government allowed this ruinous practice to continue right up to the final collapse of the Grand Banks Fishery in 1993. There's plenty blame and shame to go around: governments both provincial and federal, the two main harvesters involved in St John's and Halifax, the large numbers of fish plant processors now in the game and the fishermen themselves. If blame for the mess might be fairly apportioned, the least culpable of all in terms of plotting and orchestrating the whole wretched scheme must surely be the in-shore fishermen who gave fair warning back in the early 1980s of what was to lie ahead. For all involved, the driving force of course was pure greed as usual.

A History Lesson

The island part of Newfoundland Labrador had been only minimally colonized in the early 17th century by the French. In time they established a heavily fortified settlement at Placentia however, a place that has since given its name to the large bay in which it is located on the south coast of the Island. The fortress and the area in general remained in French hands until 1713 when, in accepting the terms of the Treaty of Utrecht, the French agreed to abandon their claims to Newfoundland and Hudson Bay. The Treaty ending the War of the Spanish Succession also gave control of the Rock of Gibraltar to Britain. The final French-English confrontation in Newfoundland occurred in 1762 at Torbay, only a scant few miles from St. John's; it seemed almost an afterthought at the end of the Seven Years War of 1756-1763. Thereafter, the French were limited in Newfoundland to having only landing rights along a stretch of the Island's coastline for the dressing of fish, (i.e. cleaning, salting and drying of cod), commonly known as the French Shore. As odd as it might seem, this right continued, at least in theory, right up until the early 20th century. By another quirk of history France still governs two small islands, St Pierre et Miquelon, that lie only a scant 25 km boat ride from the Burin Peninsula on Newfoundland's south coast. The ownership of these islands kept France an active player in the Grand Banks cod fishery until modern times.

The French Shore included, starting on the east coast, the shoreline north of Bonavista, around the northern tip of the Island and down the west coast almost to Bonne Bay. Today, there is only a small French presence on the Island in the St. George's Bay area, on the Port aux Port peninsula, situated in the south west corner of the Island. Perhaps of interest is the fact that a portion of this population includes a remnant of the Acadian population that was expelled from the Annapolis Valley of Nova Scotia in the mid- 18th century following the collapse of the Louisburg Fortress. The French were soon to lose control over all their territory in what today is modern Canada, following the fall of their bastions of Louisburg on Cape Breton Island, Nova Scotia and the final surrender of Quebec to General Wolf in 1753.

England had originally laid claim to the island of Newfoundland in 1583 when Sir Humphrey Gilbert, an adventurer planter and relative of Sir Walter Raleigh as well as a "favourite" of Queen Elizabeth $1^{st,}$ stepped ashore in St. John's and took possession of the entire island in the name of his queen and planted England's flag on the harbour's shore.

The problem of resettling the lands vacated by the French in Placentia Bay in 1713 in compliance with the Treaty of Utrecht's terms, was solved when the English 'allowed', or perhaps encouraged, several thousand Irish fishermen and their families to immigrate and occupy the area. This policy resulted in a great part of the south east of the Island including the Avalon Peninsula becoming "Irish" in character, not only in and around Placentia itself, but also throughout the land lying between the bays to the east of Placentia; Trepassey and St. Mary's, and along the entire coast line stretching from Trepassey Bay to Conception Bay including the St. John's area itself, an area now known as the Southern Shore. The last wave of (Irish) immigration came at the end of the Peninsular War (Napoleonic Wars), in the early 19th century. In effect it marked the end of all immigration to the Island. The Southern Shore on the Avalon Peninsula remains today the most distinctively Irish in culture and speech to be found anywhere on the Island. Contemporary Southern Shore people, the citizenry of St. John's included, still speak with the same Irish lilt that their ancestors brought to the area two and three hundred years ago.

The Irish (Gaelic) language itself never took hold in Newfoundland and in fact is quite unknown there today, although it was widely spoken in Newfoundland as recently as the mid-19th century. This is shown by the RC Bishop Mullock of St John's himself in the 1840s, insisting that all clerics and religious orders recruited in Ireland for his parishes in Newfoundland be Irish speakers. The Irish presently make up approximately 50% of the island's population, the same percentage as those of English stock. Located mostly on the Avalon Peninsula there are also smaller pockets of Irish found throughout the Island e.g. in Tilting on Fogo Island which was settled by Irish in the 1740s. The great majority of Irish arrived from the Irish ports of Waterford and Wexford as crew on Grand Banks fishing vessels in the 17th, 18th and very early 19th centuries. The English, arriving perhaps a little earlier than the Irish sailed out from England's Cornish West Country ports of Bristol, Devon and Poole in Somerset.

The first permanent English settlement in Newfoundland (and by extension Canada) was founded by John Guy, a Bristol merchant who arrived along with 38 other Cornishmen from Dorset and Devon, in 1610. This settlement, originally called Cooper's Cove and now known as Cupids, is a Conception Bay town about 60 kilometres from St. John's. It still proudly boasts among its citizens, descendants of those early 1610 pioneers. Recent archaeological digs in the area have turned up thousands of artefacts from the late 16th and early 17th centuries. For the most part, the people who colonized the north east coast of Newfoundland, i.e. the Bays of Trinity, Bonavista, Notre Dame and White were mainly Cornish and mostly C of E. It was these early West Country arrivals who gave the still distinctively flavoured Cornish accents to the people of these bays, to this day.

[NOTE: All settlements outside St. John's came to be commonly referred to as outports i.e. ports outside St. John's, the main port, and their inhabitants referred to, somewhat derogatively, by St John's people as "baymen"....... the baymen not to be outdone reciprocated in kind, dismissively referring to males of the city as "carner byes" and city people in general, as "townies".

The Basques in Newfoundland Labrador

In Red Bay Labrador, a 16th century Basques Whaling site was "discovered" by the Englishwoman Selma Barkham in 1977, after prolonged research stretching over a period of 15 years. Her search finally took her to live in the Basques country of Spain itself, where she remained for several years, putting together the final pieces of the puzzle to prove her initial hunches had been right all along. Her story is an interesting one. She initially became interested in the Basques presence in Canada while working on the site of the French Fortress at Louisburg in Cape Breton N S, in the 1960s. At the time, a mother of four young children, she was simply accompanying her archaeologist husband on his formal digs when his tragic sudden death at the very early age of 36 however, completely changed her life. During those early years very little financial help had been made available by Ottawa for doing her research, although it had been sought. In truth, the official Ottawa story with regard to the Basques in Canada at that time was that everything of consequence had already been collected and recorded in the Canadian archive. Following her intuition however that the archive version of the Basque story in Canada was far from complete she remained undeterred and pressed on, notwithstanding that she now had the four young children to support on her own.

From the very beginning, she had understood that it was first necessary to learn Spanish, realizing that the most important research must ultimately be done in the Basques country of Spain itself. Following a somewhat convoluted trail to reach this goal, she first spent several years learning the language, eking out a meagre living while teaching English in exchange for Spanish lessons while living in Mexico. Barely surviving on the meagre income, the family somehow managed to survive until she became quite comfortable if not proficient speaking the language. Her four children of course were completely fluent by the time they settled in the Basques country of Spain a number of years later.

By demonstrating such a high level of interest in the Labrador period of their history some four hundred years earlier, she naturally generated a lot of interest locally in Bilbao and was offered every assistance in accessing documents in government and university facilities for her research. It was here while working in the libraries of Bilbao as well as in Madrid, that she eventually found what she was looking for, by unearthing evidence of the Basques whalers' early years in Newfoundland and Labrador. European maps by the early Portuguese navigator Corte Real were discovered that clearly showed Basques whaling activity in the land then known as Terra Nova. Further research led her to zero in on the precise location of the early whaling operations on the south west coast of Labrador, in the Strait of Belle Isle, at the place now known as Red Bay. Here she was shown materials by locals that she determined were the tiles from ovens used in the rendering (trying) of whale blubber into oil. The site had indeed been well chosen by the Basques for catching the large lumbering Right and Bow head whales as they migrated through the narrow Strait of Bell Isle to warmer breeding grounds further south.

Fascinating correspondence turned up during her library researches included wills, recounting in some detail the personal lives of the early sailors and whalers during the period 1510-1580. The place itself was surprisingly large, easily the largest industrial site in all North America at the time and the seasonal home of upwards of a thousand people who came annually to engage in the whaling industry. An odd discovery of Barkham's research was the uncovering of a will from 1577 that describes in detail an ongoing dispute between two families of Galicia who were both laying claim to the ownership of a number of whale carcasses that had been left on the shore in Red Bay. Other interesting documents unearthed from 1584, describe specific work activities as well as the business interests of friends and relatives working in the new world. It was the uncovering of such documents that brought the Barkhams to Red Bay to begin their archaeological dig in the early 1970s. Locals here showed them surface artefacts that turned out to be fragments of tile from the rendering ovens that up until then had been of unknown origin. Ovens and trying pots were used only on land at this time, some two hundred years before they became permanently installed on larger stronger whaling ships, thus allowing them to remain hunting whales at sea for much longer periods of time. By the early 1980s the site of the dig had become an important archaeological site and it was only then that research funds began to flow however slowly, from the Canadian government, to support Selma's work.

On a more personal note, sometime in the late 1980s in Montreal, I was introduced to a PhD graduate student from McGill University's Archaeology Department, who was then spending his summers working on the archaeological site in Red Bay, collecting specimens for possible future museum display and to support his PhD research. I have since learned that he now resides in Red Bay permanently supervising the site as its research director. Such is the lure of Labrador. My young archeologist friend had also informed me that they'd uncovered some interesting grave sites on an island in the bay, dating from the 1570-1580 period. One burial location consisting of fourteen graves, is thought to be that of a group of whalers who in missing the final departing vessel from the whaling station for Spain late one fall, were doomed to perish during the harsh conditions encountered during their over -wintering. As well, five important whaling shipwrecks in the immediate area have been discovered and would be recovered for further study. One of these is a 1580s wreck lying almost intact, in quite shallow water within the Bay itself. From appearances fully loaded, it had gone down probably in a late fall storm, just as it was preparing to get under way for the return voyage home.

Portuguese and Spanish Basques sailors had probably been exploiting Newfoundland's whale populations, especially the Great Northern (Right Whale) and Bow Head Whale since the 1420s at least.

Basques fishermen had initially followed these marine mammals into the Davis Strait and along Baffin Island before establishing themselves permanently on Labrador's South coast in the Strait of Belle Isle, around 1510. It was a perfect location from which to intercept and capture Right Whales as they migrated through the narrow Strait on their way to warmer waters further south for breeding and having their young.

Here they had established a large whaling station where many hundreds, perhaps thousands, of Basques whalers lived seasonally, coming out in the spring and returning home in the fall. This life style was followed for most of the 16th century, until the 1580s or 1590s, when whale populations suddenly collapsed, probably from overfishing.

The name Red Bay of course derives its name from the dyes that leached into the Bay from the red roof tiles used by the Basques in their buildings. Today, one can see in addition to tiles, the remains of ovens used for trying (rendering) whale blubber and a small graveyard for whalers who either failed to make the voyage home in the fall and likely starved to death overwintering or those who succumbed to illness or injury during their six month stay working on site. There're also the sunken barks, one already loaded with a cargo of oil preparing to depart for home and others with tiles, timbers and barrel staves, or other dry goods waiting unloading, all of which are at various stages of restoration.

The Annual Visiting Portuguese

The Portuguese Grand Banks cod fishing fleet, the famed White Fleet, visited St John's annually. The vessels were so named because of their brilliant white hulls, a war time (WW2) measure undertaken to remind German U-Boat commanders of Portugal's neutrality in the war. This fleet of seventy or so vessels, mostly three mast barkentines, returned every April for their annual six months of fishing on the Grand Banks. Quite often their Grand Banks voyage was extended with a further month's cod fishing in waters off Greenland on the way home.

Because of this long 6 month fishery, most of the Fleet at some time or other, paid a visit to St. John's, usually for bait, squid being their preference, with capelin a close second. It was an opportunity to also have repairs made, to take on board fresh water and supplies, and to put ashore sick or injured fishermen for treatment. Such stopovers provided opportunities for crew members to freshen-up and even get in some personal laundering, for some might be spotted squatting beside a South Side Hills stream scrubbing a pair of long drawers and the like. Of course, football was a passion for most of our visitors as it was among the local citizenry of the city and they could be seen scrumming on the wharves alongside their vessels daily when in port or playing more formal games in our parks and even at times pitted against local squads at city pitches. Depending on circumstances, a vessel's stay in port might stretch into several weeks or so.

It was during such visits that I first heard the unforgettable beautiful haunting fado songs of Lisbon. These songs expressed more poignantly than any I'd heard before, the deep sad feelings of longing, loneliness and homesickness of sailors away from home.

After school, when I was around 12, or 13, I would often sit out on our front door step to practice guitar and sing for passersby. It was on such an occasion that I first heard the Fado, when a group of Portuguese sailors strolling by stopped to listen. Sensing their interest I invited one in their number to perform this music for us. That first listening has stayed with me a lifetime and over the years I managed to learn some of the repertoire myself. My current favorite performer of the art is of course Mariza.

The street my house was on was a familiar one for these fishermen as it lay between their vessels in the harbour and the RC Basilica (then cathedral) as well as Bannerman Park, two of their most popular destinations and deepest passions, R and R for the body and the soul. Bannerman Park was the nearest and largest public place for them to play make up soccer games amongst themselves and even on occasion against impromptu local pick up squads. In Pre Confederation times locally American and Canadian style football was quite unknown while practically everyone played soccer (football then and there).

Occasionally, as I said earlier, there might be a dozen or more Portuguese vessels tied up in port at the same time. At such times, many hundreds of their sailor/fishermen might be seen roaming around our main shopping streets of Water and Duckworth, window shopping mainly for ordinary fishermen were too impoverished to buy things in our stores. Occasionally, a top paid fisherman or salaried officer might venture into a shop to buy some small trinket or other for a child or loved one at home. Of course, the local merchant's made their profits from wholesaling bait and general cargo to the fleet.

The Roman Catholic Cathedral (now Basilica) lay just at the top of our street, a short but very steep 10 to 15 minute uphill climb from our house. The Portuguese fishermen were a deeply religious lot and our RC churches were a big draw, especially the Basilica, having just recently been elevated to Basilica status in 1955 by the pontiff. As a special gift for that honourary occasion, the Portuguese fishing industry formally presented a 4 foot high statue of Our Lady of Fatima to the Archbishop triggering a grand spectacle for us locals. A vast throng of 4000 plus Portuguese fishermen were assembled in port and then paraded through the city streets, accompanying the Madonna to her new home in the Basilica. It was a sight the likes of which the city had never seen before. She was carried along, standing atop an elevated platform, that was supported on the shoulders of a score or more fishermen marchers.

It's been estimated that perhaps as many as three thousand Portuguese sailors have decided to stay on in Newfoundland over the past several hundred years, but of this impressive number only a couple of families with Portuguese ancestry remain in the city today. All the others have moved on to greener pastures in the USA and mainland of Canada. Of course, this had become a common pattern over the centuries. The forebears of a great many present day New Englanders and other mainland parts had tried to brave the elements in Newfoundland upon first arriving in the new world only to move on, following in the footsteps of Lord Baltimore. Like him, the others too had been driven off by its harsh climate. Newfoundland's lack of schools and law courts until very late in the 18th century were also important negative factors against permanent settlement.

Loggerhead and Leatherback Sea Turtles

Tortuguero is a famous nesting site for Green and Loggerhead sea turtles on the northern Caribbean coast Costa Rica that now attracts visitors and volunteers worldwide. We had arrived during a "down" time at the sanctuary and there were no turtles of any description to be seen. Nesting females had not yet arrived from off shore to lay their eggs nor were there any hatchlings breaking through their egg shells and emerging from the sand after their 2 months of incubation.

During my travels in Australia I'd volunteered at the Mon Repos (Bagara) sea turtle rookery on Australia's Queensland coast where I witnessed the process of nest building and egg laying by Leatherbacks after coming ashore. It had been a memorable and even moving experience, one that occupied most of the night that I spent there. Leatherbacks are impressive animals both in size and behaviour and the experience you have with them will stay with you.

This wonderful ancient ocean living creature comes lumbering forth out of the breakers on a moonlit night and struggles across the sandy dunes of the beach until she chooses a suitable spot for laying. Then, using her great hind flippers like shovels she scoops out a nest, flinging sand to the side as she goes. She continues digging the pit that will be her nest until just the "right" depth for laying is sensed when she begins laying. She must not be disturbed during any part of the preliminary stages to egg laying or the entire enterprise might be jeopardised and the nest building and egg laying abandoned, with the animal returning to the sea............ It's possible she'll try again later that week but more often than not this is not the case and she'll return to sea, not to return again until the following year or even later. This is the unfavourable best guess made by marine biologists who study these animals.

Once egg laying itself begins however the female appears to enter some kind of trance like state where she doesn't seem bothered by outside disturbances whatsoever, not even by the close- up presence of people surrounding her nest during this activity. The egg laying, (there're about a hundred eggs laid usually), may take about 30 to 45 minutes to complete, after which time she again returns to a here- and –now alertness, and crawls out of the nest (almost a meter in depth, to accommodate her large bulk) and begins to cover it, again using her great hind flippers to complete the job. When this is finished, generally in less than 20 minutes, she slowly struggles back to the sea, with each push and pull along the way requiring great effort. Finally reaching the land wash, with one last mighty thrust often requiring all four flippers for the push off, she escapes the bonds of terra firma and glides smoothly into her true home, the moonlit sea, where she soon becomes lost to our view. She may not return here again for many years depending on her age, but it will always be to this exact same beach and at around this same time.

All nesting beaches have a number of characteristics in common like the angle of the slope and the sand consistency. Beyond question, the sea turtle takes fastidiousness to an extreme degree when it comes to the selection of a nesting beach. Her strange egg laying behaviour is matched only by her outstanding uncanny ability to crisscross the ocean perhaps several times, before she'll return here to lay again. During these years at sea she'll follow closely the trail of her favourite food source, the jellyfish, in particular the King Jelly, and will spend long periods of time hanging out in areas of the world's oceans where they congregate, often around sea mounts and other favourite locations. It's difficult to comprehend how such a huge powerful animal as the Leatherback can survive and even thrive on creatures that are 99 percent water, but she manages to successfully do this by consuming vast quantities of them.

Moon light is one of the most important elements involved in the survival of the species. The hatchlings are utterly dependent upon its reflection on the ocean's surface to guide them from the nest site to the land wash and sea after they break out of their shells and emerge from the sand. Unfortunately, if they become disoriented by street lights or lighting from beach front properties such as hotels, they are led away from the ocean and usually meet a sad end on a nearby highway or street.

While in Australia, I made several trips out to the Great Barrier Reef. The shorter ones were made out to Frazer Is (Great Sandy Is) in the southern part of the reef of which the latter is a popular and easily accessible destination. One takes the tour out to Frazer Is by dune buggy bus, an odd looking vehicle that takes you across many kilometers of long smooth sandy beach with little to see from the vehicle's windows other than a couple of old rusting wrecks. What followed was somewhat more interesting however; after exiting the beach the tour takes you on a long drive through a rather swampy region of huge old rain forest growth where resides the largest and most ancient ferns in the world Here we were allowed to disembark to take pictures and generally get a close up look at these curious life forms.

Deciding to move further up the coast a month later I took a Qantas flight from Sydney to Brisbane, where I transferred to a feeder 12 seat prop plane that took me another couple hundred kilometers up the coast to a rather sparsely occupied area where I rented a beach house for a week. It was an ideal place in most ways except for the cockroaches that roamed freely about in the kitchen. But with a long almost private unspoiled beach stretching out before me less than 50 meters away, where I beach combed at leisure daily and took cooling swims whenever the mood arose, cockroaches seemed like a minor nuisance. After the week here I decided to make a further 150 km trip north by bus, to a small town on the coast called Bagara, near to where I could see the Loggerhead turtles coming ashore to build their nests and lay eggs. From near here, I decided to take another trip out to the Reef as well. Spotting a nice looking B and B place in Bagara to stay from the bus window, I checked it out and ended up staying for a week. It was a week spent mostly tending to the Leatherbacks during their nightly visits to a broad secluded beach about 4km away (as described earlier), to which I hiked along an interesting but sometimes difficult shoreline. I'd leave the B and B around 5 or 6 pm and even taking time to explore along the way, usually arrived at the site around 7 pm (mid- winter in Australia), just before sundown, as things were revving up for the night's activity that lay ahead.

Officials at the sanctuary know from experience that volunteers will be needed to transfer eggs from some of the original nests dug during the night in vulnerable parts of the beach, below the high tide line, to safer locations higher up on the beach. We were told that all volunteer activity on the beach would be after dark and would be supervised by professional wild life people, from whom we got a crash course on the life cycle of these truly amazing ancient creatures.

During the night our duties involved transferring by hand, newly laid eggs from nests dug below the high water line, to higher safer nests on the beach that we ourselves prepared. Apparently, some small percentage of turtle nest building and egg laying takes place below the high tide line where they are vulnerable to flooding or even get washed away by incoming high tides or storms.

This well intentioned egg transfer programme could turn out to be something of a trade-off in the end though, for, from these newly dug nests higher up on the beach, the hatchlings will now have a greater distance to run to the safety of the ocean than before and are left exposed for longer periods of time out-in-the-open, where they become preyed upon by predators during their frenetic wild dash from the nest to the safety of the ocean. These predators and scavengers include wild dogs, ravenous foxes and other preying land animals along with hungry gulls and other sea birds then flying overhead. They all seem to have timed things exactly for the hatchings break out and are on the lookout for them as they emerge from the sand and make for the sea.

To help prevent such losses from happening, evolutionary forces have acted to ensure that most hatching seems to occur under the protection of darkness. The hatchlings, almost in unison, come clawing frenetically up through the sand on to the open moonlit beach where driven by some ancient instinct they make for the reflection of the moonlight on the ocean's surface to start their life at sea.

On the Grand Barrier Reef

Following my time with the loggerheads I decided to visit Lady Elliot Island at the southern tip of the Grand Barrier Reef on a charter from the Bagara area. After a 85 km (53 mile) trip out to the reef in moderate seas aboard a modern catamaran holding about 50 people, most of whom were young Japanese females (most of whom unfortunately became sea sick), we were served a quick lunch of cold cuts and salads at the company's small docking facility a short distance off shore. (Everyone seemed to have recovered surprisingly quickly from their sea sickness.) This was followed by an hour or so of snorkeling, available both for individual swimming snorkelers and for groups of about 15 seated inside 2 submersibles. I took the submersible for a 20 to 30 minute dive assuming correctly that it would offer a deeper, longer and more interesting adventure than I could expect to accomplish on my own.

Following the snorkeling and submersible activities we were ferried from the small 50 by 50 ft dock to a surface reef closer to the main island from where we waded ashore across a small lagoon in waist high water. Upon reaching shore many elected to swim from a sandy beach in the sheltered waters of a lagoon here, while others, including me chose to do some exploring. I struck out for the far side of the island through the brush and within only 50 meters found myself traversing a rookery of what appeared to be a smaller version of frigate birds. The up close unending loud clacks on my ear drums and the stench from their droppings lying all about almost caused me to pass out. It took me a good five minutes or more to get through the rookery to the other side. Their droppings had formed a thick spongey carpet over the years but luckily it was fairly compact so that one didn't sink in.

Another five minutes on I broke through the brush out into the sunshine and a quiet sandy beach on the far side of the island. Here, lo and behold, lying in the sand almost directly in front of me, was a young female loggerhead sea turtle, just about to begin constructing her nest.

It was a wonderful sight to behold as I'd never encountered one such as this before, so I kept my distance not wanting to disturb her. I could tell she was just about to start her digging when a noisy party of three or four others from our group broke through the brush on to the beach just the other side of her. Before I could warn them to back off they were already snapping pictures from various angles and encroaching deep inside her comfort zone.

Unsurprisingly, this sudden intrusion immediately put her off nest building and within minutes she abandoned the immediate area and slowly began dragging herself back toward the sea 50 meters away, perhaps not to try to nest again that year. I summarily told the interlopers what they'd caused to happen with their sudden intrusion, innocent enough though it may have seemed to them. I don't know if it made much of an impression on them though for they continued snapping pictures of her as she labourousily made her way back towards the breakers about 50 meters away.

Such interruptions of sea turtle nesting, (especially of rare leatherbacks), are regarded in a very dim light by authorities in Australia, as is also walking on exposed coral reefs if wearing hiking boots etc., which is very definitely a no! no! It is illegal and the culprit subject to a stiff fine.

Boston 1942

I remember many things about the year we lived with my mother's sister and her husband Jack Halley in Boston during 1942-1943. As might be expected, many of these memories are war related, then raging worldwide. My mother had taken my sister and me with her in 1942 on her trip in Boston expecting an extended stay. We crossed the Gulf of St Lawrence in mid-October on the ferry SS Caribou safely, but narrowly escaping possible death on the crossing, for on her return voyage to Newfoundland very early the very next morning, she was torpedoed and sunk by German U –Boat 69 with the loss of 136 of the 237 aboard. It made the headlines in the Boston papers but the news was blocked from publication in Canada for a couple of days.

My uncle Capt. Jack Halley had been the skipper of a beam trawler much of his life up to then, during the 1920s, 30s, (and again in the late 1940s at the end of the war). He had fished initially out of Gloucester but since the late 1920s out of Boston. Beam trawlers set their nets out over the side as opposed to stern trawlers which almost all trawlers were after the mid -1950s. In December 1945, the year of his return from active service as a Lieutenant Commander in the US Coast Guard where he commanded his own frigate, to his old fishing job, possibly the most noteworthy and memorable event of his life at sea occurred. This event took place during a major winter storm on the reefs of Sable Island, the graveyard of ships in the Atlantic.

His trawler the Breaker, was asked by authorities to attempt a rescue of the crew of her sister trawler the Gale, then foundering on the offshore reefs of Sable Island. This he managed to bring off successfully, relying on qualities of skilled seamanship, resourcefulness, courage and a love of his fellow man, which were equally matched by the herculean efforts of his loyal and brave Newfoundland crew, all of whom risked life and limb to achieve a successful outcome after a two day rescue operation. Later accounts of this rich saga produced a song of course in true Maritime tradition, the framed lyrics of which were prominently displayed hanging on a wall of Sal Bartolo's Café, 199 Summer St Boston Mass for decades. Several relics were salvaged from the Gale before she broke apart and went down, among them her brass bell and running lights, which were on display at the Fishery (Fishermen's) Museum in Lunenburg NS for many years.

Newfoundlanders in the New England Cod Fishery

It was the all -around much better working conditions in the USA that enticed many Newfoundland fishermen over the centuries to move to Gloucester and Boston in Mass. It is a fact that in the late 19th century were in great demand in the booming fishing industry of Gloucester. The majority of Grand Banks fishing schooner captains living there during the 1870s and 1880s were Newfoundlanders, as the town's municipal records show. Gloucester was then the centre of the cod fishery in New England (as was Lunenburg in Nova Scotia), as New Bedford had been for the Sperm Whale fishery during the 1820s and 1830s; with its whaling fleet in those peak years reaching the unimaginable high number of 700 vessels. Can there be any wonder that the sperm whale was almost hunted to extinction?

Many Newfoundlanders (and Nova Scotians) in the 19th century had also made their way to New Bedford to crew on whaling ships but not at all in numbers like those engaged in the cod fishery. Few fun loving family centered Newfoundlanders, unlike their stern puritan New England neighbours, could or would settle being away from hearth and home for the great lengths of time demanded by the Sperm whale fishery, many of which by the mid-19th century might last for several years. After all, cod fishing trips to the Banks would last on average only for a couple of months. On the Island of Newfoundland itself many thousands of fishermen choose to remain home and pursue the in-shore cod fishery, as exploitive as the Truck trade system was at the time. Thousands more living along the Island's northeast coast crewed aboard locally owned family schooners and spent the entire summer fishing on the Labrador coast.

Whatever, in one way or another, most Islanders were cod fishing, either on the Grand Banks, Georges Bank in the off-shore, or in the in- shore either locally or on the Labrador shore.

Working in the fishing occupation often meant starting as early as 8 or 9 years of age, which might go a long way to help explain one of Winston Churchill's instructions to the First Lord of the Admiralty at the start of hostilities in 1939-1940: "try to get as many Newfoundlanders as you can for the navy, they are the best small boat sailors in the world". This is entirely understandable, for the British Navy had been stealing fishing crews from fish merchant's vessels gong to the Grand Banks to fill their ranks for hundreds of years. They were likely the best trained seaman in the world, with a 400 year history behind them.

Many changes in trawling have been effected over the years since the 16th century when a 15 ft. long wooden log with net attached was towed behind a small sailing vessel, completely subject to wind and tide, to the behemoth modern refrigerated draggers of today. Today's trawl, with a maw that's capable of swallowing an airliner, is kept open by powerful 40 ft. wide mechanically controlled steel "doors" while along its foot, heavy metal chains hang to spook fish and drive them from their hiding places into the net, while scraping clean the ocean's bottom and wreaking havoc on the ecosystem. Most recently, large steel rollers (rock hoppers) have been added to the bottom of the net to prevent it from snagging on potentially net damaging rocks, and allowing it to access previously unattainable places along the ocean's bottom. The result is that the few remaining fish in the world's oceans are left with fewer and fewer places to hide in this desert scene. Soon there will be no places left to hide world- wide.

Back in the 1930s many trawls were still operated from the side (side or beam trawlers) of the vessel and the net required two vessels to tow it through the water between them with both steaming forward. By the late 1950s most vessels were deploying trawl nets from the stern, where the vessel can exert more effort and apply more power to the tow and from where the catch can be more conveniently passed along on conveyors to be processed by fish handlers working mid ships.

The final dagger through the heart of the fishery was its closing in 1994 by government decree. The greed displayed by all concerned: the two major factory trawler owners, (one in St John's and the other in Halifax), the owners and workers of the many newly opened fish plants, the fishermen themselves, all contributed, aided and encouraged by both federal and provincial politicians. All of them had finally beaten down a 400 year old sustainable fishery to near extinction.

The genesis of the calamity began back to the mid- 1950s with the arrival of the first foreign factory trawlers in large numbers on the Banks. Wise old in- shore fisherman predicted at the time that trouble would lie ahead for the fishery with the arrival of these monsters on the scene. Fish stocks continued to deteriorate until the universally accepted 200 mile Exclusive Economic Zone was established around Canadian waters by the government in 1974. But rather than heed warnings about catch sizes and the declining health of fish stocks, the very next year, 1975, greed won out and the overfishing by giant foreign trawlers was simply replaced by Canadian owned (monster) trawlers and business continued as before, if anything on a scale even more intensive than before. This state of affairs continued until there was little left to catch, resulting in the closure in 1994.

A large percentage of the island's working population (some 40,000 to 50,000 fishermen and allied fish plant workers were affected directly) was thrown out of work by the fishery collapse. Large numbers of these unemployed fishermen later became gainfully employed as we sailed past workers in the oil fields of Alberta, where they supplied the much needed muscle in that industry. In the meantime, the population of Newfoundland continued to decline from a peak of around 580,000 to around 505,000. Most recent tallies show something of a rebound however, putting the number at around 518,000, with the increase in large measure due to the Island's own recent oil industry boom that has also brought with it a new sense of pride. Most alarming however, as it could negatively affect future government social programmes, Newfoundland has declined from the province with the largest number of children per family in Canada to that with the fewest. There're simply aren't enough people left in the province to pay for the social programmes any more.

In Cod We Trust.

Cod (as well as other cold water bottom feeders like Haddock, Halibut and Turbot), once present in their billons, lived out their entire life cycle from egg, larvae and fry to adult and old age on or near the rich shallow banks that lie off the south east coast of Newfoundland, undertaking only minor migrations, usually inshore to chase their major food source capelin, during their spanning in June. They have now virtually all but disappeared.

For the sake of maintaining good trading relations with certain European countries, the Federal Government had allowed large modern, processor factory ships along with their feeder trawlers, to continue fishing, completely unregulated, throughout the 1950s, 60s and 70s until the 200 mile EEZ was established in 1974.

Thereafter, they continued fishing, now legally, outside the EEZ i.e. around the Nose and Tail of the Banks until caught in the act of poaching inside the zone and brought to court in St John's in 1994 only months before the closure of the fishery. Unfortunately for the cod, when the feds finally got around to ridding the waters of the monster foreign ultra-modern factory trawlers with the declaration in 1974 of the EEZ, they seemed to think that the fishery could continue as before with only the role of the principle villains changed.

Regardless of the many alarms sounded by fish demographers at Newfoundland's MUN and most notably by Dalhousie University's much esteemed Ransom Meyers in Nova Scotia, (prior to his appointment at Dal, Dr. Myers had also spent many frustrating years working for the federal fisheries department, where his research had been largely ignored), the Grand Banks overfishing was allowed to continue unabated. The Government of Canada, in refusing to accept even their own in -house fisheries' experts' reports in the final years, (where there was now finally good science being produced if still very poor politics) allowed the unregulated fishery to continue, until they were finally forced to put it on life support by declaring a moratorium in 1992 and finally a complete closure in 1994. It had finally reached a point where there were simply no more fish to catch!

Ocean Conservancy

At present, sharks, a species at the top of the food chain, seem to be one of the most threatened in the world's oceans, with alarmingly low numbers of these animals remaining. In a related manner I'm reminded of an incident from my boyhood, an encounter with a large shark, though a very dead one. While I was beach combing along the shore below the cliffs of Conception Bay one day, I suddenly came upon a great commotion of people circling around a 25 foot basking shark, a marvelous animal that neither they nor I had seen before. Apparently the animal had become entangled in a fisherman's salmon net, practically destroying it, and dying there from revealed causes. The fisherman had somehow managed to drag the whole mess ashore, where it now lay for all of us to wonder at. The basking-shark is a large animal but not a carnivore as are most of the commonly known sharks, but feeds on plankton like whale sharks and baleen whales. It has been traditionally exploited as a food source in many parts, along with its fins and oil for other reasons, reasons that have finally put it on the endangered animals list.

Within a day or two of its landing and subsequent discovery by the media, a large number of the citizenry from nearby St. John's soon arrived on scene to take photos and get a close up look of the unusual fish, which would have been a rare sight indeed. The group included a number of local Chinese Restaurant owners, who soon busied themselves cutting off the shark's large fins, for use as the main ingredient in their establishments' shark fin soup. The fins likely would have also been frozen and some sent to restaurateur friends abroad. That was 60 years ago and it may also have been necessary to salt and dry some of it if wishing to ship it abroad to friends later, in bulk.

Shark fin is hugely popular in Asia because of the erroneous reputation it has as a powerful aphrodisiac, a property it does not possess. But the primarily Asian demand for it remains great regardless which has led to an alarming decline in shark populations worldwide. This in turn has triggered alarm bells to go off among ocean ecologists because of the shark's important position in the ocean's food chain.

The Scourge of By -Catch (the by- kill)

The ocean is fast becoming an ocean of jellyfish due to the sharp decline in the number of sea turtles over the past 50 years, an animal that feeds almost exclusively on that creature. Among the top culprits causing this high turtle mortality are plastic bags, which are eaten by the animals mistaking them for jellyfish. The plastic bag pollution of the ocean is also becoming a major cause of population reduction in many species of seabirds.

"By- catch" or more accurately, the by-kill, are the millions of animals that get caught "accidently" in the thousands in drift nets, each stretching for 50 miles or more across the ocean that are now so commonplace in industrial fisheries. Equal to drift nets in contributing to this mortality, are the thousands of long lines that also can stretch for 50 miles or more in the ocean, each line armed with millions of baited hooks that are attached to separate lines that hang every few feet along the main long line.

These nets and lines, are set out ostensibly to catch specific species of fish, but catch in addition to the targeted animal, large numbers of unwanted species, commonly called the by- catch, which may include species as diverse as sharks and sea birds, all of which are hauled aboard (usually dead or near dead), and then thrown overboard. Adding to their built- in inherent dangers, these huge drift nets are also frequently abandoned after becoming badly damaged or lost in storms. In this condition they are left to continue their deadly fishing unchecked, acquiring in so doing the apt macabre name of "phantom" nets. In time, these abandoned nets become heavy with catch and sink to the ocean bottom, where they are emptied of their contents either by scavengers or by natural decay, at which time they rise again to the surface to continue their phantom fishing, continuing the viscous cycle until the net rots away.

As an example, a trawl net set out for a targeted catch of snow crab or yellow tail turbot, may result in that species being only one third of the total catch in a net that also brings aboard tonnes of untargeted species, (astonishingly, estimates range anywhere from 10 to 100 lbs. of discarded by-catch for every pound of the targeted species that eventually goes to market), including rays, skates, sharks and many others, all of which are then discarded.

A similar kind of carnage is also occurring on the sea bottom by bottom trawlers among the living creatures that reside there, including as well deep water corals. These trawls, with 200 ft wide mouths kept open by massive steel doors, are towed across the sea bottom bulldozer like, rolling along on giant steel balls with the catchy name of rock hoppers, that take the net into places previously unattainable where they now catch animals that previously could remain out of reach. There is literally no place to hide on the ocean bottom.

Here, an entire world of living organisms is being destroyed that includes sponges, sea urchins, sea stars, anemones, shell fish and corals. Left In place of this rich unique ecosystem, a moonscape of sandy desert is left behind. During the past 50 years the ocean has been depleted of 90% of its large fish species: Blue fin tuna, swordfish, marlin, sailfish and shark, while becoming a reservoir of jellyfish.

Arctic Issues

I was introduced to Inuit people and their culture for the first time during the first of several summers I spent working for the Fisheries Research Board (Arctic Unit) in the recently settled hamlet of Whale Cove, a small community of less than 100 people situated on the western shore of Hudson Bay, between Rankin Inlet and Arviat (previously Eskimo Point). It was 1962 and I was sent there to collect specimens of canine teeth for population studies from Beluga whales that I captured in the area. At the time of my arrival, the 100 or so people living in the Cove had themselves only recently arrived as the first settlers for this Government experiment. The site had been chosen because of its traditional importance to Inuit as a good place for hunting the abundant wildlife in the area from arctic hare and foxes to beluga and seals.

The Whale Cove residents had come from two different groups of people representing two entirely different life styles: one group had been "taken" down from Coral Harbour to the north, a hamlet on the archipelago islands where seals were the major source of clothing and food, while the other group had been representative of the nomadic caribou hunting people who inhabited the tundra lying inland to the west of Whale Cove. These two groups nevertheless seemed to my untrained eye to have meshed very nicely at the time of my arrival perhaps only 3 or 4 years after the village's start up in the late 1950s, as a part of the government's then modern resettlement plan.

Wilfred Grenfell- Missionary Doctor to Newfoundland Labrador

Before 1962 I had seen very few Inuit, in fact just once before. That was during the summer of 1947 when I was a boy of 12, and the place was St Anthony, a growing settlement on White Bay's great northern peninsula near the tip of the Island. My father had taken me with him on what was to become an unforgettable voyage of discovery, aboard the coastal steamer SS Northern Ranger that serviced the isolated outports along the coast of Newfoundland and southern Labrador. St Anthony had grown over previous decades to become the administrative centre for the Grenfell Mission Association in Newfoundland, under its energetic and dynamic founder Sir Wilfred Grenfell, a medical missionary from the UK, a man endowed with a ton of gumption, who had come to Newfoundland/ Labrador in the 1890s as a volunteer- employee of the Royal Mission to Deep Sea Fishermen. From rather humble beginnings he had grown the Grenfell Mission in less than thirty years into an internationally known charitable foundation through a mix of personal moxy, determination and drive.

The Inuit I saw that summer day in St Anthony had come to receive medical treatment or to visit relatives at the large new and, for that time, very well equipped modern hospital Dr. Grenfell had built there. It was the Grenfell Mission Association's imposing showpiece in 1947. Indeed this splendid hospital would remain as Sir Wilfred Grenfell's most important contribution to the health and wellbeing of the isolated fishing families living along the Island's northern peninsula and Labrador coasts until the 1950s when it was finally taken over by the provincial government of Newfoundland.

Labrador's most northern (now Nunatsiavut), Inuit inhabitants had been evangelized by the Moravian Missionaries as early as the late 18th century. These devout but very practical evangelists had come to stay on that harsh coast in the 1770s, after initially reconnoitring the area 20 or 30 years before. In communities lying mainly north of present day Hopedale they laboured until the 1950s, when control of their entire missionary enterprise was also finally relinquished to the provincial government. Until then they had provided educational, (including even musical training on brass instruments and choral singing), effective farming techniques, building skills and medical services, along with their bible studies to the Inuit along that part of the coast. They were a sturdy and practical group of missionaries, originally from Czechoslovakia, who'd come to Labrador very well prepared to undertake their work in that tough environment. Ramshackle remnants of their time there remain in the form of decaying frame school houses and churches, long abandoned root cellars and even vestigial vegetable gardens.

They were so effective teaching English in their schools that it was said that literacy among the Inuit of northern Labrador in the late 19th century was probably higher than that among Newfoundland's outport fishermen; not to mention their playing Haydn and Mozart pieces on brass instruments and their singing of choral pieces.

During the 1919 influenza (Spanish Flu) epidemic that swept worldwide, Labrador's Inuit population suffered huge losses from which they only slowly and marginally recovered.

It was at St Anthony, centrally located to the region of his activities near the Strait of Belle Isle, that in the 1920s, Sir Wilfred decided to build his modern hospital, to provide modern medical services, (later the Association diversified to include educational and co- operative activities as well as establishing an orphanage), to the inhabitants along those harsh isolated coasts. Although at the beginning servicing only fishing families locally around Indian Harbour, he within two years, expanded by adding two fellow London trained doctors and nurses. Soon there were several small cottage hospitals along the east coast of White Bay and by the 1910s he had expanded the original mandate of the Mission to include indigenous Inuit people in southern Labrador. It remained a privately operated NGO until the late 1950s when it finally relinquished control to the Newfoundland government, just a few years after the Moravians had done similarly.

The Inuit I saw that August day visiting their relatives at the Grenfell Hospital certainly made a memorable impression on my 12 year old imagination, clearly standing out in their traditional seal skin clothing and knee high skin boots. I can remember still one short stocky fellow carrying a hunting harpoon slung over a shoulder as he ambled by puffing on a pipe.

I have already written at some length in my memoir Molasses Bread and Tea, about the unforgettable summers I spent in Whale Cove, a newly settled Northern Affairs experiment of less than 100 Inuit. I recall the chain smoking unilingual Segu, my assistant during my first summer there and young Solomon Voisey, my amusing 15 year old and completely bi -lingual assistant who made my second year in Whale Cove a whole lot more comfortable. There were three Voiseys in Whale Cove at that time: Solomon, his mom Rosie, who also was a great help to me and his older married brother Lewis. These three were descendants of early 19th century Voisey settlers on the Labrador coast, where their name now graces a large bay on provincial government maps, thanks to the recent discovery of huge, rich deposits of nickel and other valuable minerals in the area.

(The Voiseys must have been on the western Hudson Bay coast many decades before my visit as well, for I remember the skipper of the long liner with whom I hitched a ride south to Whale Cove from Rankin Inlet in 1962 drawing my attention as we sailed past to a patch of bright green vegetation still quite visible on the tundra as being the site of the outhouse of the original Voisey homestead.

Climate Change

Climate change (global warming) was of course an unheard of threat during the years I was working in Whale Cove. Much of the Arctic Ocean was still solidly frozen over throughout even the summer months and any hope of getting freight delivered into Whale Cove before July was out of the question and one couldn't set out fishing nets for arctic char or beluga until late June at the earliest. Most people still followed the traditional occupations of hunting and fishing, having only recently been coaxed by the federal government to abandon their old migratory life style and settle down in a permanent community.

Only a few scant years before my arrival, small units of these people were still living under canvas or skin tents during the summer months and even snow houses in winter or possibly in some facsimile of sod and stone shelter near larger centres. In Whale Cove, they now formed a community of 100 people, housed in twenty five or thirty government provided prefab one room shacks, perhaps 20 by 20 ft in size that had been set up in a semicircle ringing the cove. Barrels of oil and gas were shipped in during July or August for use as fuel for winter gas for outboard motors. As they were emptied of oil, the barrels served both as family garbage incinerators and storage containers for cut up beluga caught during the summer and used as dog food through the winter. This is how the community was when I stepped ashore from the long-liner that first year.

During those years, I was working and living nomad like, for the Fisheries Research Board of Canada (arctic unit); roaming from one assignment to the next, usually in the eastern arctic, Hudson Bay and the North West Atlantic; sometimes at sea, sometimes camped out on the tundra or if lucky, put up temporarily in a vacant bunkhouse on land.

I had just recently completed 3 months at sea, collecting harp seal canine teeth on the Newfoundland (Labrador) seal hunt aboard the M.V. Theron, followed by a couple of months back at our labs on Pine Ave W. in Montreal, preparing and analyzing slides of these tooth specimens and preparing for the Whale Cove assignment. This routine had been a repeat of one that I'd untaken the year before. Before that, there had been a stint at Dildo, Trinity Bay in Newfoundland collecting pilot whale specimens and a couple of years before that there'd been short trips to the Grand Banks to get samples of Red (rose) fish.

The job was generally enjoyable often seemed ideal, for one who liked a sense of adventure and working on one's own as I did. As well, at the time I didn't mind traveling around a good deal of the time, be it on ships, long liners or bush planes. Then, working among Inuit people was always a great pleasure, besides, they liked my guitar playing and singing. Most days held wondrous adventures and at the end there was always a clear open starry sky presenting a light show of swirling, wildly dancing northern lights.

Nunavut

Nowadays, climate change talk is at the top of almost all agendas in the north as it should be, seeing as people here, as with with the low lying atoll dwellers of the south Pacific, seem to have the most to lose in the short term. Yet, there is still a wide diversity of opinion being expressed among the Inuit people themselves, stretched as they are across Canada's wide northern longitudes. It sometimes seems a conflicting and confusing debate, particularly as it relates to the possible harmful effects that weather may be having on wildlife and other arctic resources.

Many Inuit worry that their very lifestyle may be at risk in this gamble with climate. Even our southern ears have recently picked up on the noisy difference of opinion being expressed between the eastern and western arctic regions with regard to the effects of climate change on polar bear populations.

For example, the outlook on Baffin Island in the east was not at all optimistic about the survival of polar bear populations in their area, whereas, on the other side of the country, there was nowhere near the same sense of alarm being expressed in this regard.

Nevertheless, where that animal now seems to be in trouble or will be shortly, wild life officials and hunters alike are pressuring Government to put measures into effect to protect the species; perhaps even to declare the polar bear endangered, as it is in the USA, although in that country it is not for reasons necessarily being due to climate change alone.

There are now four distinct areas making up the Inuit occupied lands in Canada's arctic. These four regions moving east to west are: Nunatsiavut (NL), Nunavik (PQ), Nunavut, and Nunatsiaq (NWT). The most easterly district, Nunatsiavut (Our Beautiful Land), with a population of about 2,000, is basically the northern half of Labrador and is the smallest of the four in area. Its immediate neighbor to the west is Nunavik, (Great Land), with a population about 12,000 that encompasses the northern third of Quebec. Lying next to the west is Nunavut, (Our Land), by far the largest and best known region of the four and is to some degree self -governing. This huge middle section of the country, comprises most of the country's arctic and sub -arctic regions, including the whole of Hudson Bay and has the greatest population at 33,000, among the four regions with a capital at Iqaluit. The most western area, Nunatsiaq, (Beautiful Land) lies within the North West Territories. In Nunavut there is prevailing and widespread belief among hunters that climate changes are already well under way. Here, they now see an alarming melting of sea ice earlier in the spring and a later freeze –up in the fall, all due to global warming. There is now also the appearance of flora and fauna, never before seen in the region. There is widespread general agreement among the population that there are climate changes occurring here now and these changes are becoming a source of growing local concern. Nunavut's capital Iqaluit, population about 4300, the old Frobisher Bay, is now the largest town in Canada's entire arctic.

However, at this writing, there is much less concern being expressed with regard to effects of climate change on polar bear populations moving west from Nunavut to Nunatsiaq. Around Tuktayaktuk on the Arctic Ocean for example, the opinion of hunters and others, supports the belief that at present there is no noticeable decrease in polar bear numbers. Nor is there any great alarm being expressed with regard to a noticeable decrease in thickness of seasonal sea ice here.

So what are we to think? We have the Inuit in the east saying one thing, and the Inuit in the west saying another with regard to noticeable changes in their environment due to global warming (climate change). Abroad, there have also been warmer temperatures measured in waters north of Norway than in Canada's eastern arctic.

But if true, if climate changes were to occur across the entire arctic in a big way, they would certainly bring about dramatic changes to the Inuit life style, affecting transportation, hunting, diet, recreation, education and so on. Supporting the arguments being expressed in Nunavut, hunters note that sea ice in recent years has been thinning, making it more dangerous to hunt from this traditional platform for polar bears and Inuit alike.

It is these same Inuit hunters who point to the much shorter period of hard sea ice that's now available for polar bears to hunt seals from, as a possible cause for their decreasing numbers. As a consequence, these animals are now forced to spend more time on shore scavenging for food, often going without while awaiting new ice to form in the fall. There is also growing concern for polar bear cubs that are thought to be incapable of swimming the increasingly greater distances in open water between shrinking ice floes. As evidence, they offer the growing number of very young polar bear carcasses that they notice being washed up on shore. Many mother bears also appear to be dangerously thin and less able to fend for themselves and their young. This situation is quite noticeable among polar bears along the western shore of Hudson Bay, especially around the town of Churchill Manitoba, a location where polar bears traditionally spend the late months of fall foraging on shore awaiting the freeze-up, a freeze-up that now comes later each year. Adding to the confusion here, Churchill's town dump also acts as a magnet, further encouraging these "resident" bears to spend longer and longer periods loitering in the area then in years past.

Global Warming

Meanwhile overall global warming is becoming increasingly accepted; most recently, thanks to striking satellite imagery showing that the Arctic Ocean's ice pack has been steadily diminishing in thickness and area during the past 20 years. Latest measurements show the ice pack has now receded 200 miles from the shoreline compared to only 50 miles, 20 or more years ago. These mileages are the measured distances from the shorelines of Canada's Arctic Archipelago to the (ice) floe edge taken in midsummer when the warmest temperatures are observed and the maximum distances are realized.

This distance represents an expanse of open water that is thought by polar bear wildlife experts, to be too great a distance for polar bear cubs to be capable of swimming (as evidenced by the ever growing number of cub carcasses found washing up on arctic island shorelines) and possibly even too great a distance for weakened mother bears to manage as well. In this regard, the growing expanse of open water is perhaps also indirectly responsible for reducing the number of denning bears on land, as well as the number of adults feeding on seals out on the ice floes.

The Grenfell Mission Association ......unique to Newfoundland

As mentioned above, one of the most extraordinary men to toil on the shores of Newfoundland and Labrador was the Englishman Dr. Wilfred Grenfell. He first arrived as the sponsored agent of the National Mission to Deep Sea Fishermen, founded in 1881, (it received a Royal designation from Queen Victoria in 1896), providing a system of care for migratory fishermen living apart from their Newfoundland outport community homes for much of the year, generally from April to October, while pursuing the Labrador Fishery and living aboard their schooners. He had arrived in 1892 and for the first year had worked only locally in Indian Harbour but son expanded. Over the years he accomplished much: By his retirement in the late 1930s he'd built up the complex, philanthropic organization (NGO) that still bears his name.... ...... After just a year or two with the Mission he'd launched his own career that in time delivered medical care, along with educational and social welfare programmes, to the thousands of isolated fishermen and their families scattered along the extensive northern coastlines of the Island and the lower half of Labrador.

England's oldest colony, at the time of his arrival in 1892, Newfoundland was a self -governing (1854) colony, soon to be dominion (1905). Later knighted for his work, after setting up his own altruistic society 'the Grenfell Mission Association' he soon became a familiar figure on the lecture circuit in high society circles of Montreal, Toronto, Chicago, New York, and many others, touring constantly, drumming up both funds and volunteers to finance and assist the work of his growing mission. These volunteers were the globe-trotting peace -corps youth workers of their day, who came to work for his mission in Labrador during the early decades of the 20th century. He married in his mid-forties a wealthy Chicago woman as well, thereby further strengthening the Association's resources.

The Moravians in Northern Labrador (Nunatsiavut)

The Moravians had arrived on the Labrador shore a century earlier than Grenfell, in the 1770s, but had remained on the northern half of the coast, (now Nunatsiavut) ministering exclusively to an Inuit population. Both philanthropic organizations came to wield enormous influence over successive Newfoundland governments over the years, beginning as activities in Christian missionary evangelism, but expanding over the years into areas of education, social welfare and health (areas where there had been historically NO or very little government involvement until the 1940s in the case of the Moravians and the mid -1950s for of the Grenfell Mission Association, when they finally relinquished control over their valuable properties to the provincial government. Throughout the 18th and 19th centuries for all intents and purposes there had been little or no formal Newfoundland government involvement in the lives of most Labradoreans, from its far off capital in St John's. For instance, the largest public hospital (and probably the largest building), outside of St John's and Corner Brook, i.e. the Grenfell Association Hospital in St Anthony, was not turned over to the Newfoundland government's Health Dept. until the mid- 1950s.

Dr. Grenfell was a very active medical practitioner and tireless advocate for his mission, a man who could be found out on a dog sled run attending to some medical emergency, (requiring perhaps a two or even a three day absence from his St Anthony head-quarters), or away on the stump, drumming up support on the lecture circuit in the major cities of Canada and the North Eastern US. Thanks to this advocacy, his medical mission became very well- known amongst the glitterati of his day and he himself something of a celebrity. From local newspaper clippings of that period he appears to have been a favourite among wealthy American bankers and powerful industrialists. His calls for financial aid and influential volunteer support seldom went unanswered. Many young aristocrats of the time, including Rockefellers, Vanderbilts and Roosevelts, saw it as an opportunity to be philanthropic while at the same time offering an opportunity for adventure and exploration in the wilds of Labrador, which was then considered something of a final frontier in North America, an adventure perhaps on par with an African safari or travel in South American.

Dr. Grenfell had several very dangerous close calls himself while out on these emergency dogsled runs. One in particular made such an impact on him that he wrote an account of it in a spellbinding booklet that he published under the catchy title "Adrift on an Ice Pan" (1909) that was a best seller and is probably still available.

George Cartwright was a scot who accomplished many wonderful things during his three decades working as a Factor for the HBC in Labrador in the mid -18th century, before returning to live in England. During one transatlantic crossing he mentions rather disdainfully striking up an acquaintance with fellow passenger the American turncoat Mathew Arnold.

Donald Smith was another major Scottish Hudson Bay Factor who spent twenty years in Labrador before moving on to greater things in Canada where he became President of the Bank of Montreal and later President of the Canadian National Railways. He was also a Principle of McGill University during these years. He's the man shown in the iconic CNR photograph driving home the last spike at the completion of CNR's railway line in British Columbia in November 1885. While toiling for the HBC in Labrador he grew in hothouses many different kinds of hard to come by vegetables to show local Inuit that such things were possible even in Labrador's harsh climate.

Ocean Conservancy Issues

In a 2006 UN General Assembly meeting, on the table there was a proposal to introduce a global moratorium on deep sea bottom trawling, a method of fishing highly destructive to sea bed habitats and its abolition had gained widespread support in the Assembly. The measure came within a whisker of passing that day at the UN, where however, consensus decision making processes are followed, making specific proposals more difficult to pass, and it was vetoed at the last minute by Iceland's delegation. A nation of only 300,000 people thus killed the introduction of a protection critical to the survival of deep sea life. Such small minorities of course should not be allowed to torpedo the fate of life on the planet. In such circumstances the science is the easy part, what are needed are men and women of political skill and tenacity to see that such measures get passed in such UN votes.

George Bush's very surprising valuable actions with regard to ocean conservation when he established numerous large marine reserves in the South Pacific were implemented late in the final year of his presidency. Such a philanthropic good will gesture, while having gone largely unnoticed, was still very important. With one stroke of his pen the total area of marine protected reserves world -wide were practically tripled. These latest reserves were all located on remote widely dispersed islands in the central and South Pacific Ocean which may account for the relative obscurity of his legislation.

Brazil leads the world in sea turtle conservation efforts thanks to the heroic efforts of TAMAR (Projeto Tartarugas Marinhas....Marine Turtle Project) that has successfully released 8 million hatchlings to the ocean........all five species nesting on beaches in that country are included in the project.... Loggerheads, Leatherbacks, Green, Olive-Ridley and Hawksbill.

Mexico is also a leader in providing sea turtle sanctuary. Encouragingly, most recently, Japan has now banned commercial activities it previously has been engaged in, like trade in turtle leather and turtle shells that had benefited its traditional cottage industries, in eye glass frames, shoes, purses etc. Ghost fishing by abandoned or lost drift nets continues to be a huge hazard to sea turtles as well as many other marine species.

It's thought that the Norseman Leif Erikson, son of Eric the Red, led a group of Icelanders to North America around 1000 CE and set up a small settlement near a place now known as L'Anse aux Meadows only to abandon it for unknown reasons after perhaps only ten years, before returning to Greenland. We can only speculate as to why their attempt at settlement failed. Along with the long harsh winters and relative scarcity of food encountered here, another possibility might be that they were met with unaccommodating and unwelcoming aboriginals that resulted in on- going hostilities during the brief period in which they were there. It is also quite unknown who exactly these aboriginal peoples might have been. They could have been the indigenous people of Newfoundland, the Beothuk, but these people are thought to have been quite peaceful; on the other hand it might have been the Innu or even Inuit people from across the Strait of Belle Isle in Labrador. As mentioned previously, it is thought that there were probably no more than one hundred or so Norse settlers in the group at any one time, during their 8 or 10 year period occupying the location. It's also possible that it might merely have been a trial or temporary experiment at colonization on their part, in order to see if permanent settlement might be feasible there. From appearances it seems as if they had come for the long haul though, for the place was equipped with what appears to be a fairly sizable smithy's forge, to make and repair tools and weapons. Additionally, there appears to have been a special spot on the beach where a primitive dry dock might once have been in operation; a place where either long ships or the wider freight carrying Kroners, could have been hauled up for repair

Iceland's "Cod -Wars"

It could have been different for the Newfoundland Fishery If Canada had more closely followed the example of Iceland with regard to protecting its fishery. That small island nation in the North Atlantic with only some 320,000 inhabitants, acted with considerably more muscularity and much earlier in the game than did Canada in defense of its fishery. As early as the 1950s, just a few years after gaining its independence from Denmark in 1947,(Note: Newfoundland chose to join Canada and not go it alone in 1949) it set up its first 10 mile limit to help protect local fishing grounds from foreign overfishing. Quite quickly that fishing limit was soon extended to 50 miles in the early 1960s. The main challenge to this new limit and Iceland's tough talk was made by British trawlers that had come to regard the waters around Iceland as their own private fishing preserve over the centuries. Britain continued to fish within the 50 mile limit initially but now with Royal Navy frigates providing security for the trawlers. The Icelanders weren't cowered by Britain's show of force however and reacted in kind by sending out their own heavily armed patrol gunships to enforce the newly enacted law. The naval skirmishing between the two that ensued came to be known somewhat grandiosely as the "Cod –Wars". Very little damage was inflicted on either side by all of this posturing however but Iceland's message got through loud and clear and the cod-wars were soon brought to an end with Iceland winning the day. Emboldened by this victory, the country then increased its EEZ to 100 miles and again in the early 1970s to a whopping 200 miles. The time seemed to be right for a such drastic move to be taken in 1974, and soon all maritime nations were getting on board, including Canada.

Unlike Canada with its mixed resource economy, Iceland had only its fishery to depend on, to Iceland it was everything, the very economic lifeblood of the young nation. It was its sole resource and only industry, and had acted accordingly.

[Note: Unfortunately, self- interest can sometimes be taken a bit too far as mentioned earlier, when in a recent decision taken in 2008, Iceland vetoed a near consensus vote of agreement in the UN that would have put a halt to deep sea bottom trawling in its surrounding waters. It was a desperately needed consensus vote of agreement for the sake of seabed bio-habitat survival that failed to pass, thanks to Iceland's veto].

Canada's lack of fisheries muscle remained intact until the Liberal government's Ministry of Fisheries came under the purview of a tough minded Newfoundlander named Brian Tobin in the mid-1990s, who in a very convincing no-nonsense manner quickly arrested a Spanish trawler caught fishing illegally in Canada's exclusive economic zone and towed her into St. John's harbour to face charges of illegal fishing. (The charges were subsequently dropped as were Spain's somewhat legitimate counter charges against Canada, of committing piracy on the high seas).

I might add that at the time of this international dust up I was traveling in Spain, and had been staying for several weeks in the attractive port city of Alicante on the Mediterranean coast. My local fish monger, having gotten to know me a little by this time, asked off handily one morning where I came from. As it happened, it was just about the time of the arrest of the Spanish trawler in question. Upon learning that I was a Canadian, and from St John's no less, he broke into gales of laughter and gleefully announced that our two countries were almost in a state of war over the arrest of the trawler. I hadn't been aware of the international incident that was unfolding in my home city and asked him to expand on the press headline. He, being a proud and clearly separatist Catalan, could care less about the fate this Spanish trawler and was reveling in the distress of the central government in Madrid. Upon learning this, I too felt comfortable enough to join him in a good laugh at Madrid's expense. I would have been a great deal more circumspect of course had I been in Madrid at the time of the telling.

WW2 St John's

It has been said about the city that during the war years, it seemed a much more exciting place to be than before 1939. The city now seemed to have about it a kind of nervous energy that was absent before. To its inhabitants, the first sounds of early morning were now not those of squabbling sea gulls fighting over some discarded fish entrails thrown by fishermen into the harbour but the piercing hooting whistles of RCN and RN corvettes as they prepared to hook up for or return from convoy duty in the North Atlantic, part of the famous North Atlantic Squadron. There were always a dozen or more of these fast and mobile little convoy life savers in port, vessels that the townsfolk soon became very familiar with. From St John's they steamed out to join the main body of the convoy that had departed Halifax's Bedford Basin a day earlier, a huge flotilla made up of many more escorts and hundreds of freighters loaded down with war material and food for Britain.

I remember seeing these corvettes tied up at wharves, sometimes several abreast, along the south side of the harbor where they were clearly visible from my 3rd floor bedroom window. Also, from our house on Victoria St. we could easily hear the clatter of the hob nailed boots as companies of young soldiers and sailors (accompanied usually only by a single kettle drummer), marched up or down Prescott St., a short block from our house, on their way to or from guard duty at installations along the waterfront.

Many of the older downtown St. John's streets were still cobble stoned in those years, greatly amplifying the sounds of passing traffic. Horse drawn carts with steel or iron rimed wheels were particularly noisy. Horse shoes and hob nailed boots all made their contribution to the general ruckus of the street. The Emperor Nero had cobble stones removed from the roadways around his favourite palace for the same reason apparently, replacing them with wooden logs.

In St John's, shortly after the war ended, our cobble stones were taken up, along with the city's street car tracks, to open the way for gasoline powered buses, to the chagrin of many.

Whenever I heard troops marching by, I'd run out hoping to catch sight of them as they marched down Prescott St on their way to harbour front. We lived at the bottom of Victoria St., a street that ended in a terrace with a steep tier of steps that led down to Duckworth St, a major east west business thoroughfare. The terrace afforded me a wonderful front row seat to all the city's major parades that inevitably marched along Duckworth St, often involving a thousand or more marchers, from all the major services including their brass bands. After the USA entered the war and its Newfoundland bases became operational, contingents of their military from USAF Pepperrell and USN Argentia would also take part in these marches. Sunday mornings were often busy times for the military, when perhaps several hundred of the lads would be mustered out, many with hangovers and marched off accompanied by a brass band, to attend some church service or other sometimes with the Governor in attendance, or perhaps to provide an honour guard for some visiting royal or ally dignitary.

From 1942 until the US bases in Newfoundland closed in1968, many of Hollywood's best known stars and celebrities had at some time or other had passed through on USO tours to entertain the troops, and excite the locals. Included on this list were Frank Sinatra, Phil Silvers, Marlene Dietrich, Johnny Weissmuller (Tarzan), Bill Cosby, the Four Aces and Steve Lawrence. Elvis also sang a few tunes for the locals on his way through to Germany. Even John F Kennedy had reason to drop in at the US's Argentia Navy base on one occasion when his famous PT Boat 109 needed repairs. Some show biz celebrities had even been stationed at local bases, John Williams, (airman 2nd class), the Oscar winning composer of mega hit film scores and conductor of the Boston Pops, made quite an impact locally during the almost 4 years he spent in St John's (1952-1956), moonlighting on the side as a pianist and composer with his Star Lighters musical combo, while still finding time to score the local tourist films

"Happy Union", and the much better known "You Are Welcome ", a 22minute film based on local folk melodies, for the Newfoundland Tourist Board.

During the 25 years the bases existed in Newfoundland, some 30,000 local women married US servicemen and left the Island, (most permanently), for residency in the US, including two of my paternal aunts, thereby strengthening an already very strong bond between Newfoundland and the USA. To many poor local young women the US was a land of riches, Cokes and Camel cigarettes. As might be expected there was strong rivalry between the US servicemen and the local lads for these fair maidens, local lads whose counter was "if you can't get a man get a yank". Many a parent of our young girls was deeply suspicious of the swagger and bravado of the glamourous yanks as well, with all their superior 'back home" talk. With all this competition going on many a fistfight broke out in the clubs and on the streets of St. John's as well as other centres i.e. towns like Placentia, situated near the US Argentia Navy Station and Stephenville a small town near the huge Harmon USAF base, which was at the time the largest USAF base outside the continental USA.

Other celebs who had purely pragmatic reasons for coming by our shores were aspiring first time transatlantic aviators, who came by to scout out suitable jump off locations for their first transatlantic flights. Newfoundland witnessed both the successes and the failures. The successful flyers included Alcock and Brown, Charles Lindberg and Amelia Earhart. Ms. Earhart made two successful flights from Newfoundland, on the first in 1928 as a passenger, in so doing becoming the first female to make the crossing, while on her second in 1932, she became the first female pilot to make a solo crossing of the Atlantic.

The famous Mayflower with the Pilgrims aboard also made a quick stopover here for water and supplies, on its way to New England. Lord Baltimore tried out the place as well, in Ferryland, for a couple of years, but moved on to Baltimore, Maryland, after a decade or so, finding the local weather too inhospitable. Jacques Cartier had a good look around the Island's west coast "the French Shore", before continuing on to the Maritimes with his map making activities, where he made the following comment, "two acres of Iles de La Madeleine are worth the whole of Newfoundland". Good publicity for the place outside of cod fishing, appeared to be hard to come by from the beginning, with respect to settling the Island.

Yet again, on the other hand and in more recent times, the celebrated travel writer Jan Morris has said of St. John's........"one of my favourite cities anywhere..."

....before continuing with the following steam of adjectives, from which you can pick your choice ....."windy, fishy, anecdotal, proud, weather beaten, quirky, obliging, ornery, fun"

.... Tourism is now a major industry, with a wild growth in whale and ice berg watching recently. This fortuitously helps make up for the collapse of the fishery in 1992 and more recently the tanking of crude oil prices. The tourism department of late has struck gold selling the Island with a stunning and on-going collection of TV ads emphasizing the wild unspoiled beauty of the place and its eerily mysterious but enchanting geography.

But on the Avalon alas, especially in the St. John's area, the trends of commerce are definitely ultra –modern and high tech. The sprouting of unsightly cookie cutter housing developments around the city, and a proliferation of super highways interspersed with ultra -modern satellite shopping centres all seem to detract from what many a tourist is looking for, however satisfying to the local need.

Summary of the Cod Collapse

The principle reasons for the collapse of the cod fishery on the Grand Banks in 1992, so stated, follow, listed in order of importance.

Foreign (over)fishing: This continued on the Toe and Nose of the Grand Banks as well as on the Flemish Cap, after the 200 mile limit had been established in 1974.

Overfishing by Canada: (Nova Scotia and Newfoundland): overfishing by local companies with far too many factory trawlers and fishermen, all looking for far too few fish...... Locals simply took over the overfishing where the foreign trawler operators had left off after the EEZ was enacted in 1974. This in turn led to far too many fish plants being set up and far too many fish plant workers, reaching the embarrassing stage eventually where it became so tempting that young people abandoned high school in droves to take jobs in fish plants short term, just long enough to qualify for UI eligibility.

Bad science: Hopelessly inaccurate computer models attempted to account for what was really going on but totally missed the mark. .... It became a classic example of garbage in/garbage out and to a large extent may have been politically inspired.

Even worse management: Collusion by both levels of government, federal and provincial. An Ottawa - St John's conspiracy existed.

Cold Water: Possibly a contributing factor but not very likely.

Seals: the old reliable was still being included in the mix.

The Outport Slaughter House

It was during a Christmas vacation spent at the modest family farm of my Uncle Dick and Aunt Liza Stapleton that I was first exposed to the butchering of cattle and pigs. The family had a licence to operate a small slaughter house and butchered less than a dozen animals a year, mainly pigs along with a couple of steers generally. The slaughter of a steer, or heifer, bull or cow for that matter, can be a disturbing thing to witness at any age, and especially so for a twelve year old. I was around that age when I saw my first and only animal slaughtered, and it was anything but pleasant to witness. I still remember practically all the horrid details as if it was only yesterday and they remain among the most disturbing I've ever witnessed. I include here even the incidents I saw during my years collecting specimens for the Fisheries Research Board of Canada (Arctic Unit) at the pot head (pilot whale) drive in Dildo, Trinity Bay NL, and the traditional NL harp seal hunt (though excluding the white coat kill) and several summers spent in the arctic catching beluga whales with Inuit hunters. So I don't think it's a matter of just being squeamish, although I confess to tending in that direction by nature.

I guess the whole incident in question came about because I simply wanted to be regarded as 'one of the boys' (although much older ones than I) in the Stapleton family, with whom I spent most of my school holidays between age 10 and 14. I may have volunteered but it's possible I was 'invited' by someone to be one of the slaughter house team that day. My assignment was "to save the blood", a position at the very bottom in the pecking order.

My entire previous experience at having anything to do with animal slaughter consisted solely of one day seeing my Aunt Eliza pith a hen with a long metal knitting needle which certainly appeared a lot more humane to me than seeing its head cut off at the chopping block and watch mesmerized, as the headless creature ran around the farmyard for a minute or two before collapsing in a bloody heap. Once or twice I had also very reluctantly accompanied my father into our basement to observe, as he drowned a litter of unwanted kittens in a large enamel pail of water. Mercifully, on these occasions he had quickly covered the pail with the lid to spare us both from having to actually see the drowning

I remember while passing the Stapleton barn one morning hearing a pig squeal loudly and went inside to investigate. Here I beheld my one eyed Uncle Dick standing in the pigsty attempting to knock out a pig with wild swings from a 10 or 12 lb sledge hammer. The animal was making a hell of a racket, squealing in terror, as it attempted to avoid the sledge as Uncle Dick tried but without much success to trap it into a corner for a knockout blow. Uncle Dick then well over seventy, had lost the sight in one eye years before in a carpentry accident, so wasn't quite as skilled in the business of slaughtering pigs as he might have thought. At the moment I entered, he was lurching about in hot pursuit of the terrified pig that kept avoiding him, by darting quickly from side to side, and corner to corner. Uncle Dick, wielding the heavy sledge was taking wild swings at the animal's head but kept missing, as the wily animal was very quick on its feet and kept escaping the blows, all the while continuing to squeal at top volume. The spectacle was both frightening and comical and I was more than relieved when Uncle Dick finally ordered me to go fetch my cousin Leo who lived next door, to come kill the pig. Among the two Stapleton families with 8 or 9 men still living at home, Leo was the only one legally licensed as a butcher and shortly after arriving he quickly brought an end to the horror show.

Just a few meters away from Uncle Dick's house stood the now seldom used carriage house. One side of this large space was still referred to as the carriage house, and still housed two beautifully maintained horse drawn carriages. The better looking one was painted an emerald green with beautiful, delicate, gold leaf lettering bearing the owner's name. It was outfitted with a couple of well -padded leather seats up front, for easing the trips over bumpy unpaved roads to and from "town" on market day, about 12 miles away, and for making occasional trips to mass on Sundays. It had the best quality springs available, locally made at Fever's Forge in St. John's. The light weight wheels with beautifully slender spokes ran along on firm wheel rims wrapped in pliable but tough rubber. But it was only used for special "dress up" occasions now, like funerals and weddings, or going to mass on occasions for which Aunt Liza's presence might be expected. These were the only times in fact she now seemed to bother getting dressed up for even go out for that matter.

On the other side of the carriage house was the slaughter house. This room wasn't getting much use by now either, except in winter when the Stapleton's slaughtered a small number of their own cattle and pigs. During the rest of the year, it remained for the most part unused, a space only where men might sometimes congregate to get in out of a shower of rain or where a man might perform some special task like sharpen an axe, scythe or saw on the large mounted hand turned whetstone kept there. The lofts in the carriage house were still filled with remnants from the long gone days of the fishery: salmon nets, a cod trap, a couple of killicks i.e. stone anchors enclosed in a wooden cage, some wooden buoys, a few small anchors and mismatched oars. The smell of fish was now weakening but it still maintained a lingering presence. Signs of a newer occupation in farming were just beginning to take over in the place.

Slaughtering a Steer

In the centre of the slaughter house floor there was a small trap door, covering a space just large enough to hold a 2 or 3 gallon water bucket. Next to the trap door was a heavy cast iron ring anchored firmly into a thick spruce floor board. A number of strong heavy iron hooks were bolted into the room's exposed heavy overhead beams, where sides of dressed beef or pork from just slaughtered animals were hung, to get them ready for display and market. Hogs, after slaughtering, were shaved of their course body hair in an extra -large wooded tub that was filled with boiling water for that purpose and placed just outside the slaughter house door for easy access. Just before slaughtering began, an extra -large empty water bucket was placed in the trap door space to catch ("save") the blood from the animal after its throat had been slit for bleeding out after being knocked unconscious by a blow to the head from a 10 lb. or 12 lb. sledge hammer. After the butchering, dressing and a general cleaning up of the place, a large quantity of the blood collected earlier was used to cook up a fresh batch of black puddings (blood pudding), which were then hungrily gobbled up by the assembled family crew.

The animal to be slaughtered was usually tied to a fence post near the slaughter house door a day prior to slaughter, where it remained unfed, usually bleating, for 24 hours until its hour of doom arrived, when it was "led" into the slaughterhouse. By this stage it seemed well aware that something very much out of the ordinary was going to happen, and its bleating reached a fever pitch as it was being pushed into the slaughter house, unnerving us all. To any observer it would be impossible not to feel sympathy for the animal at this time.

On the occasion in which I was involved, during the usual run up to the slaughter, when the bleating animal, a steer, was tied up to the fence post outside, I became a bit too sorry for its fate and threw it an armful of hay, thinking of it as a last supper perhaps. Unfortunately, just as I was in the act of performing this forbidden act of kindness, Uncle Dick suddenly materialized on the scene.

Showing not a smidgen of sympathy he grabbed the hay away from the feeding doomed beast and instantly blew his top. He could be quite scary at such times and luckily for me Aunt Liza was there to come to my rescue at that time.

On the appointed day itself, the slaughterhouse was made ready with the necessary tools for the butchering: the heavy sledge hammer, a number of sharp knives for skinning and saws for dressing the carcass later, the water bucket for saving the blood, strong hemp ropes and block and tackle for raising the animal to the ceiling for final dressing. I remember growing very apprehensive as proceedings were about to get under way and at that moment I regretted having gotten myself into such a pickle. This feeling of anxiety was not just in relation to my blood "saving" role but concerned the whole scary business in general. It was just at that very moment that I was told to take up my station behind the trap door with the empty water bucket and place it in the space provided. Stern warnings from Leo followed with instructions to kept it steady during the butchering, to prevent any spillage during the animal's death throws that would follow its being knocked down and 'stuck' and the blood was flowing freely.

I was initially proud of having been given this job to do on the slaughter house team. After all, wasn't my volunteering to do it all about my wanting to be considered a grown up like all the others on the team? Even if it was just a menial job the lowest one in the pecking order, it was still an important job, one that certainly had to be done by someone, if not by me then by someone else. I was a boy of 12, a boy longing to be thought of as a man like my mature cousins and I couldn't wait to make that happen fast enough. But alas! It was at the very moment when things were about to commence, that my courage threatened to fail me completely. I felt an uncontrollable urge to bolt from the slaughterhouse and escape into the fields.

Leo, our next door neighbour Uncle Mike's eldest son, then in his early thirties, was the go-to-guy on the slaughter house team, the one in charge of operations among the 4 or 5 Stapleton men then on hand. When it came to butchering, there was little doubt about who was the captain on the bridge of our slaughter house ship. All the others fell into their various backup roles almost naturally, by habit I assume, as their various assignments turned up.

It was Leo who swung the heavy sledge. This was something I found the most shocking to behold and seemed almost too shocking to be witnessed. Uncle Dick's son Edward seemed to be next in order of importance on the slaughter ship, the first mate, and it was he who next sprang into action, knife in hand, with the animal now lying on the floor, with its legs jerking spasmodically. Straddling the beast he quickly struck with the knife, thrusting it with great force deep into the animal's neck, and in one firm sweeping motion drew the razor sharp blade across the wide bovine throat, from which the blood began to spurt like a geyser from its severed arteries. All this horrific action was transpiring directly in front of me, less than a foot away, as I squat transfixed griping the water bucket with a hypnotized vice grip. As there had been no rehearsing for this drama, nor, for that matter had I ever seen anything remotely like it before, I was left almost speechless and frozen with a combination of fright, shock and awe.

Even after the passage of 70 years, I still shudder with the memory of it. I can still visualize it all so clearly and in almost every detail, just as it happened on that very day: the animal being (pushed, pulled or dragged) into the slaughter house by 3 or 4 of my grown up male cousins.....the continuous awful bleating and bawling out it makes in protest to what must certainly be apprehension and fear of what lies within. ....I see even the length of thick manila rope looped around its horns that soon will be used to tie him down closely to the heavy iron ring in the floor, beside the trap door...............then, after he's tied down he's now so close to me that we're almost nose to nose, the intimacy of this so shames or embarrasses me that I'm forced to look away, beyond him, out through the open door toward the spruce forest just beyond the yard. But there can be no escaping this reality now, our fates are sealed. The actions now unfolding proceed with frightening speed and a practiced efficiency. I somehow manage to remain calm enough to concentrate on my duties. Everything goes as smoothly as possible.

Any feelings of fear or empathy that still lurk, even the panic that had invaded my thoughts just a few moments ago, I have suppressed..... I sense an increased concentration by everyone involved, an increased focusing on their roles as the drama unfolds. There is no joking or small talk, among them now! I've become mesmerized by everything yet I wonder if I will be able to hold out until the end or if I'll bolt and run at some dreadful point yet ahead.

I manage to get myself into a squatting position beside the trap door and take a firm hold of the water bucket with both hands. I am only a couple of feet in front of the doomed animal's head. We make eye contact momentarily again and I wonder if he recognizes me as the human who gave him a handful of hay only the day before .... a time and place that must now seems a world away. I try to calm myself with prayer and await the unknown still ahead.

I'm startled alert again as the wretched beast is forcibly turned around a little to get it more in line with the swing of the sledge being practice raised by Leo. Just for an instant our eyes meet again, this one last time. I can almost feel the uncomprehending fear within them. His head is now tied down securely by the short length of rope to the iron ring in the floor. What can he be possibly thinking? When everything seems ready, Leo lifts the sledge high above his shoulder and swings down with one mighty blow. There seems to be a slightly dull muffled cracking sound like that made when walking on snow on an extremely cold day when the sledge slams into its target, dead centre on the animal's brow, and he collapses forward, first on his knees, then topples over on his side. As he goes down our eyes meet again but I know I am only a ghost figure to him now. My eyes are immediately drawn to a large patch of purple discolouration that has suddenly appeared in the centre of the animal's forehead and rapidly radiates out, discolouring the once attractive brown and white mixed coat of a healthy steer. I almost pass out after seeing these transformations and at that moment realize I would if I could, get up and run, but I'm completely paralysed with shock and so I continue squatting, frozen to my post. He crumbles before me convulsing slightly, down to his knees and then tumbles over on his side in a tragic heap. There is a brief moment of almost reverent silence around the room, before Edward leaps forward and delivers the coup de grace, driving the sharp six inch blade deep into the animal's neck and makes his cut in one sweeping strong motion.

Now, two others, Frank and Jim, throw their arms across the animal's forelegs and breast area to steady the shaking there and attempt to maintain in position the geyser of blood spouting strongly from the neck into the water bucket. At this point, the animal's head is now practically resting in my lap and I concentrate with all my might, on holding the bucket upright and steady, beneath the torrent of blood pouring forth. The flow continues like this for some time, before easing up to eventually become a trickle, at which time all hands encircle the animal and begin to apply pressure to its carcass, the rump, flanks and abdomen, poking, prodding and pushing, forcing the remaining blood in these areas to drain through the gaping neck wound.

When they feel that this has been accomplished, they disembowel the animal and complete the work by skinning it. One can finally detect an almost palpable sense of relief amongst those in the slaughterhouse and the conversation again starts to lighten with a more relaxed day- to -day kind of banter. As the butchering is done in wintertime, it's been quite cold in the slaughter house during the operation, but after the animal has been opened up and its warm innards spill out onto the slaughterhouse floor a heavy cloud of steam rises above the carcass and the room temperature rises. It's finally over and I too can at last feel some relief at having survived the experience. But I notice that my hands have begun shaking with the release of the tension. There's a lightness of spirit in the group, almost a giddiness among them now. They even start to joke amongst themselves again as they go about their final mopping up chores.

When I return to the slaughter house sometime the next day, I find the carcass has been nicely dressed out: now skinned and disembowelled with all the important organs taken away, I see only two cleaned longitudinal sections of carcass hanging from hooks in the overhead rafters. These reminders from the previous day's horrific drama are almost pleasant to look; two spotlessly clean, attractively dressed sections of beef, now ready to be inspected by meat market proprietors who'll soon be coming out this way from the city. There are no real reminders here of the rather gentle creature I had tried to feed just the other day. For a moment I feel a sad melancholy overcome me. The blood that I'd so carefully collected in the large water bucket has long since been cooled, cooked expertly with milk and onions into blood puddings by Aunt Eliza and devoured by the crew. They've smelled quite good cooking on the stove and have disappeared just as quickly as she's put them on plates in front of her 'byes' who've crowded in on benches around the kitchen table.

The End

Biographical Note

Newfoundland writer John P Christopher, musician, writer, marine biologist, sits down to Second Helping to continue his anecdotal accounts of growing up in wartime St. John's and Newfoundland outports in the 1930's, 1940's and 1950s that he began in Molasses Bread and Tea, where he also detailed his observational and collecting studies of harp seals, beluga and long fin pilot whales while working for the FRB of C in the arctic.

Bibliography and Sources used in the Newfoundland Labrador Nunavut Memoir 1942-1967.

Circling the Midnight Sun.........James Raffan

Cold Recall (Reflections from the North West Passage)..........Roald Amundsen

Ships of Discovery and Exploration…....Lincoln P Paine

Ships of the World….....Lincoln P Paine

Moby Dick........ Herman Melville (Born 1819. Died 1891)

The Cruise of the Cachalot....... Frank T Bullen

The Grand Banks (a pictorial essay)........ Jean Pierre Andrieux

The Vikings (a short history of) ....Jonathan Clements

Atlantic .... Simon Winchester

Who Killed the Grand Banks? .... Alex Rose (MUN)

Captains Courageous .... Rudyard Kipling

The Sea around Us........................Rachel Carson

Silent Spring ....Rachel Carson

The Unnatural History of the Sea .... Callum Roberts

Ocean of Life .... Callum Roberts

Sea of Heartbreak: Michael Dwyer (NL fisherman memoir, with F Mowatt citation)

A Tall Fish Tale (Gloucester) .... Mark Kurlansky

The History of Cod .... Mark Kurlansky

St John's in World War Two .... William Rompkey

Whales of the World (A sea guide to:) .... Lyall Watson

Sea People (Changing Lives and Times in Newfoundland Labrador) Editors.........
Helen Woodrow and Frances Ennis

A Whale for the Killing.....Farley Mowatt

West Viking........................Farley Mowatt

People of the Deer .... Farley Mowatt

The Other Side of Eden: Hunters, Farmers and the Shaping of the World).............
Hugh Brody

The Sea (Mission Blue).......................Sylvia Earle

The World is Blue (How our fate and the oceans' are one).....a TED Talk......
Sylvia Earle

Shackleton's Dream (Fuchs, Hillary and the Crossing of Antarctica)..... Stephen
Haddlesey

As Near to Heaven by Sea (a History of Newfoundland).......Kevin Major

Sea Sick: the Global Ocean in Crisis........Alana Mitchell

Beyond Words: What Animals Really Feel and Think ....Carl Safina

The Voyage of the Turtle........Carl Safina

Song for the Blue Ocean.........Carl Safina

Molasses Bread and Tea (a personal remembrance of outport Newfoundland life, the last days of the traditional Newfoundland seal hunt circa 1960 and an account of capturing beluga whales with Inuit hunters in the Arctic: circa 1961) ....John P Christopher

The New York Times Book of Science Literacy Vol. 2

The New York Public Library Science Desk Reference

The History of the Decline and fall of the Roman Empire...........Edward Gibbon 1776

On The Origin of Species................. Charles Darwin 1859 (born 1809 died 1881)

The Reluctant Mr. Darwin.....................David Quammen

Darwin ....Texts, Backgrounds, Contemporary Opinion, Critical Essays.... Selected and Edited by Phillip Appleman 1970

Various PhD. Theses, research papers and articles as they relate to the story of Portuguese whaling and cod fishing in Newfoundland and Labrador waters during the 15th, 16th and 20th centuries......

A review of the English/Irish Migratory Cod Fishery to the Grand Banks from Wessex ports during the 17th, 18th, and 19th centuries.

the author makes no 10 on the North Toronto Post magazine
announces its list of the10 best things to do in Toronto. Dec 2004

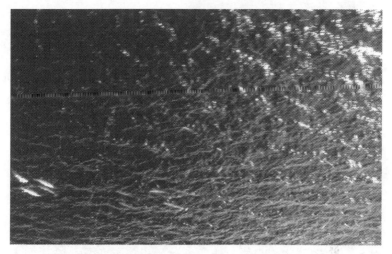

aerial view of beluga whales migrating on the surface of Hudson Bay. June 1962

author sitting on the side of freighter canoe on the Whale Cove
beach, District of Keewatin NWT (now Nunavut). August 1963

female beluga fetus, approx. 32 cm in length. Whale Cove August 1963

author reading from Molasses Bread and Tea at book
launch in Annapolis Royal NS August 2006

unknown Inuk man standing on shore of Hudson Bay near Whale Cove 1963

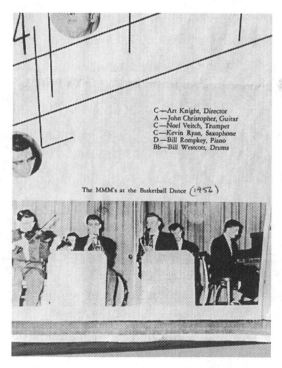

founding members of the Memorial Music Makers
band at work St John's NL 1956

aerial view of beluga whales swimming in formation
just below surface of Hudson Bay. June 1962

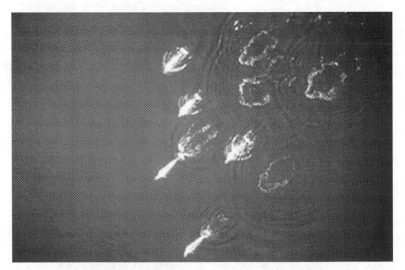

aerial view of beluga whales swimming in formation while
just breaking the surface, Hudson Bay June 1962

sea turtle on the Great Barrier Reef off Queensland Australia Dec 1996

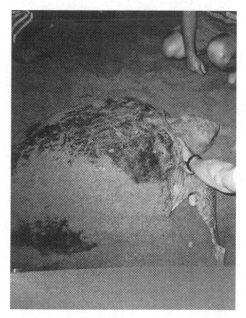

loggerhead (?) sea turtle nesting at Mon Repas
(Bagara), Queensland Australia Dec 1996

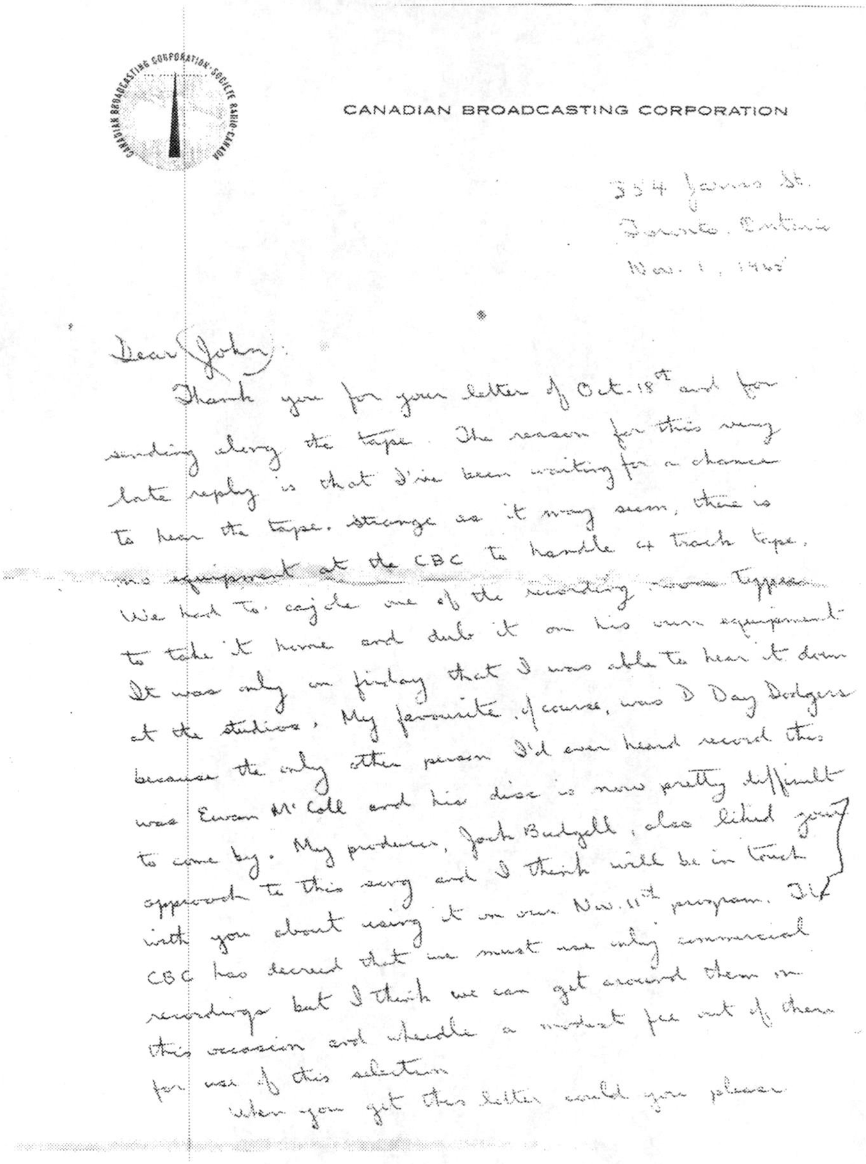

CANADIAN BROADCASTING CORPORATION

354 Jarvis St.
Toronto, Ontario
Nov. 1, 1965

Dear John:

Thank you for your letter of Oct. 18th and for sending along the tape. The reason for this very late reply is that I've been waiting for a chance to hear the tape. Strange as it may seem, there is no equipment at the CBC to handle 4 track tape. We had to cajole one of the recording room types to take it home and dub it on his own equipment. It was only on Friday that I was able to hear it down at the studios. My favourite, of course, was D Day Dodgers because the only other person I'd ever heard record this was Ewan McColl and his disc is now pretty difficult to come by. My producer, Jack Budgell, also liked your approach to this song and I think will be in touch with you about using it on our Nov. 11th program. The CBC has decreed that we must use only commercial recordings but I think we can get around them on this occasion and wheedle a modest fee out of them for use of this selection.

When you get this letter could you please

a letter from CBC"s famous "Rawhide", Max Ferguson, to the author re the author's debut on national CBC radio Nov 1965

CANADIAN BROADCASTING CORPORATION

I give Jack Budgell a call at the CBC (WA5 3311) since he has no phone number by which to reach you. By the time you call him he should have cleared permission from the CBC to use the song.

Sincerely,
Max Ferguson

a letter from CBC''s famous "Rawhide", Max Ferguson, to the author re the author's debut on national CBC radio Nov 1965

a loggerhead (?) sea turtle returning to the sea on Great
Barrier Reef off Queensland Australia Dec 1996

a waterfall tumbling into Western Brook Pond fjord , Gros Morne Sept 1994

author about to board Beaver float plane to begin aerial
survey of beluga whales in Hudson Bay. June 1962